The Soul Speaks

by Zara Marselian

The Soul Speaks
First Edition Published October 22, 2010
By La Maestra Publications

Written by Zara Marselian
Edited in part by Deborah Hergor
Cover and Illustrations by Candy Cuevas

To God for the inspiration

*To those who have so willingly
offered to open their hearts
and share their experiences*

*To all of those souls still facing adversity,
trying to find a new beginning
in this wonderful country*

*To my children Lena, Sonia and Leo,
whose ancestors faced many challenges
arriving to and in this country*

About the Author

Zara Marselian is the CEO and co-founder of La Maestra Community Health Centers and La Maestra Foundation. A native San Diegan and child of refugee and immigrant parents, she founded La Maestra to provide healthcare and social services to the immigrants and refugees in inner-city San Diego. Since 1990, La Maestra has expanded to serve patients in several areas of San Diego, including City Heights, El Cajon, National City and Lemon Grove.

Zara has been recognized locally and nationally as an ambitious advocate for the cause of helping the uninsured and improving access to culturally competent health and social services for the diverse communities of San Diego. She has received many local awards including the 2002 Kaiser Permanente "K-Star Award"; the 2003 "Channel 10 Leadership Award" and the 2004 "Channel 10 Overall Leadership Award"; the 2004 San Diego County "Health Heroes Award"; the 2004 Latino Builders' "Community Service Award"; the 2005 "Making a Difference for Women Award" and the 2006 "Woman of Accomplishment Award" from Soroptimist International of San Diego; and the 2009 "Excellence in Health Services Award" from Chaldean and Middle-Eastern Social Services.

In 2004, she was one of ten leaders in the nation to receive the Community Health Leaders award from the Robert Wood Johnson Foundation. That same year, she was honored in a special Statement for the Congressional Record by Congresswoman Susan Davis for her efforts and accomplishments at La Maestra. And in 2007, she received The Greenlining Institute Lifetime Achievement Award in recognition of her vision and leadership in healthcare.

Table of Contents

Introduction

The stories in this book were brought together to share the human experiences, the hopes and dreams, the struggles and determination, of human beings around the globe and to document the atrocities done by humans to others that cannot be ignored. The writings build awareness by recounting these real life stories, exposing readers to what "reality" is for people with different backgrounds, cultures and beliefs. Readers will see distinct patterns which link these real-life human stories, despite the fact that they come from diverse areas of our world. This realization builds connectivity among all of these characters and others worldwide. These stories also bring hope to others who have lived, or continue to live, in survival mode. These are their stories, their interpretation of their own experiences; validation of facts was not the focus. La Maestra hopes this will serve as another means to achieve our mission of advocating for the overall well-being of all humans.

The reader begins to identify with the immigrant and refugee characters by experiencing their physical and emotional journeys. Emotions, dreams, willpower and Spirit transcend any religious, cultural or political boundaries. We start connecting as humans to humans. The name of the book could be Tapestry of Life: a Compilation of Real Life Stories or The Soul Speaks. It tells how the culmination of will leads to survival, and how communities develop at this grassroots level, one human experience at a time. All of these stories involve visioning and spiritual aspects.

The soul speaks, permeating through language, through cultural, political, religious beliefs; through experiences. It is heard throughout the world and universe. We are all connected through our soul as it surpasses the ego. We communicate on a different level through our souls. The soul knows truth, recognizes other souls, regardless of what the exterior looks like. The soul sees the silhouette of another soul and recognizes immediately the essence, needs and sufferings. Language, verbal communication, is not needed in this interaction. It is only our minds that distract us from responding based on reasoning we have been taught. If we let our souls communicate, pay attention to that information and act accordingly, then we, as a human race, can create peace.

What is the difference between the soul and the spirit? I believe that the soul is the core, cumulative, old, unseen essence of our being. The spirit is the energy sent out from the soul. It is what reflects the color, the depth of our souls, transcending our bodies and our minds. Take, for example, the nonverbal communication which occurs in the waiting rooms at the La Maestra Community Health Center in City Heights. Mothers from many diverse cultures sit with their sick children. They look at each other, recognizing, empathizing, with the other's situation. They cannot communicate in the same language but their souls are talking and reaching out at that survival level.

I've often asked myself what draws each of these human beings who have been through a lifetime of suffering in survival mode to work in community development. On the outside they look like others but on the inside they have scars. They are the "walking wounded". I feel so honored to have been part of their lives, knowing them, respecting their life experiences. It is with this spirit that I come to share the stories of how they have suffered, survived and now thrive, filled with the determination to help others at the community level.

I wish to thank all of the "thrivers" who have consented to share their life experiences in this book. As they began to recall what they went through, many cried. Each one said that they had pushed away their painful past, buried it deep down in their cellular memory. After a few meetings, they began to recall all the good feelings and experiences which were locked away along with the negative ones. By the time we finished annotating their lives, I could feel that a definite transformation had occurred in each of them. It was amazing. It's as if, through the documenting of their life experiences, their suffering, pain and joy were acknowledged, validated and brought into the light of their present lives. What began as a painful process ended with some degree of healing. I respect the courage, willingness and trust that each of them demonstrated by sharing their life experiences and bringing hope to others who are still working through their own past. This was truly an honor for me to serve as the annotator of their human experience.

The following is a list of some of the topics and issues covered in The Soul Speaks. All of them have significant effects on health and overall well-being.

Acculturation
Alcoholism
Career Goals and Opportunities
Children with Disabilities
Courtship and Marriage
Culture, Values and Traditions

Oppression
Piracy
Political Upheaval
Politics and Health
Poverty
Public Housing in the US

Detention Camps
Discrimination
Domestic Violence
Education
Escape
Faith
Family Dynamics
Gender Roles
Hope
Human Rights
Human Trafficking
Inequality
Lack of Essentials
Mental Health

Refugee Camp Life
Religion
Religion and Health
Rights of Refugees and Immigrants
Rites of Passage
Self-Help & Self-Empowerment
Spirituality
Suicide
Superstition
Survival and Determination
Torture & Rape
Traditional Medicine
Trauma
War

Alexei's Story

Akara

Alexei stepped through the opening of his family's hut to view a beautiful and expansive horizon. The vast landscape was dotted with bushes and acacia trees. Flocks of swallows and robins flew in formation above the village called Akara, which means "fork in the road". Akara is 260 miles due north of Kampala, the capital of Uganda.

In 1949, in this village of about fifty people, Alexei was born. Alexei's mother was helping to harvest their family's crops when her labor began. Alexei was born beneath the shade of an acacia tree. Alexei's mother had birthed twelve children, but only half would survive to adulthood. By the time Alexei was born, most of his five surviving siblings were grown, married and living in surrounding communities. There was a forty year age difference between Alexei and his eldest brother and, when Alexei made his entrance into this world, he was lavished with nurturing and love as the baby of the family.

Alexei's family lived in four mud huts, all with grass-thatched roofs. His father had engineered a rock foundation in the main hut, which was unique in those times. The foundation served to deter wild animals and curious reptiles as well as to provide a barrier against the run-off from the heavy rains of March through July, referred to as the rainy season.

Alexei's father had two wives. His second wife shared two of the huts with Alexei's half brothers and sisters. It was not uncommon for men to have more than one wife, as long as they could support them and their children. Although marriages were not arranged, it was customary for the groom's family to examine the reputation of the intended bride's family before the union took place. As with Alexei's mother, only seven of the thirteen children born to his father's second wife survived. Alexei's half brothers and sisters were closer in age to him than his full siblings. The youngest half brother was only a year older. They all lived together harmoniously as one large family. Alexei's father split his time between both wives in

10

their respective huts. Jealousies between the wives and families were not apparent to Alexei until after he was grown and began to hear rumors of discontent. The second wife moved away to a further hut.

Both wives came from the same tribe, called the Acholi, which means "black people". The Acholi tribe had originated in Sudan, moving south into Uganda long before Alexei was born. The tribal language is Acholi, believed to have originated from a main ethnic Luo language spoken in northern Uganda, around Kenya's Lake Victoria and along the Tanzanian border.

Aunts and uncles would journey to visit during the dry season, and Alexei remembered one aunt in particular. She was a medicine woman, and Alexei would follow her around learning about the herbs she collected along with their various uses. In addition to medicinal uses, the herbs were used in cooking and during rituals and celebrations.

Every household had a shrine made of rock formations. The shrines were placed just outside the entrance to each home. Villagers danced in front of the shrines to celebrate significant life events. For example, the death of a chief or significant elder was celebrated over a long period of time, concluding with a special dance, the *Bwola*, performed primarily by men to the beat of the Acholi drums. The women have a dance of their own, called *Apiti*, and would often join the men dancing the *Bwola* to conclude the funeral rites. During the dry season there is a courtship dance called *Larakaraka* or *Omik*, which means "elope". The *Dingi Dingi* dance is a very colorful dance performed by both men and women as part of a ceremony to greet dignitaries. The women's movements are so graceful that they look like they have no bones in their bodies. *Otole* is the war dance in which men dance with spears and shields to demonstrate their strength and ferocity. Alexei's mother had markings along her waist as a symbol of beauty, though piercings and body markings were discontinued during Alexei's generation. Alexei saw the dancers and tribal members wear paint during the ceremonies, but the designs were temporary.

Although the tribal members grew up with these rituals and ceremonies, they were not a part of any religion. It was only later in her life that Alexei's mother was baptized as a Christian. His father never converted to Christianity or Islam.

Alexei's given name is Ochola. The tribe does not carry a family name. His siblings called him different pet names, and it wasn't until Alexei entered elementary school in the third grade that he selected a Christian name for his first Holy Communion. The elementary schools were run by Catholics and Anglicans, so the children knew about Christmas and Easter and celebrated both in school.

The main village celebrations started at the beginning of the harvest, with the most important holiday being New Year's Day. By then the crops had been sold and there was money to buy gifts and clothes. They celebrated with food from the bountiful crop harvest, homemade wine, singing and dancing. Men and women danced together, with the exception of the *Apiti*. Domestic animals were slaughtered for the feast, and hundreds of tribal members attended.

Alexei's family had communal work arrangements during the planting and harvest seasons. All family members would participate. Shifts were organized to clear crops before sunrise, and again later in the day. Schedules were drawn up according to the size and type of crop, and payment came in the form of food and wine at the end of the long day. No one expected cash. There was always ample land for farming. Titles weren't issued for land, but it was available for homesteading to those willing to work. Cotton was the primary cash crop. It was a tedious process preparing the soil for the cotton seeds, and then planting them in straight lines with precisely measured spacing. Cotton crops required weeding two or three times a season. The harvesting of cotton was just as time consuming, requiring picking, sorting and bagging before the cotton could be sold. Alexei's family also cultivated peanuts, sesame, millet, sorghum and a variety of vegetable crops. Harvesting occurred during the dry season when the temperature was upwards of 90 degrees Fahrenheit. When Alexei's father was not working in the field, he could be found carving stools and handles for knives. He also raised tobacco for his personal use.

Alexei's tribe hunted during the dry season, mostly deer and rabbit, with spears or bows and arrows. One of Alexei's uncles specialized in trapping leopards, valued for their skins. He was admired for his skill and bravery. Alexei learned early on to respect the creatures that roamed the land, including lions, rhinos, and buffalo. Alexei and his half brother tended the family's cattle and goat herds. They stayed alert at the river's edge, watching for crocodiles lying in wait for the herds coming to drink. Snakes and scorpions were also a prevalent threat.

Every member of the tribe had a role and responsibility in their communal structure. Alexei was told that before his parents' time, their tribe had been part of royalty. If they had continued with this structure his father would have been a chief. Alexei's father was highly regarded by his tribe. After teaching himself to read and write, he had worked as a local administrator—all the while maintaining the family's farm and livestock.

As a child Alexei viewed his father, who was called Ogal or Obyac, as a strong, calm man, of slender build, not very tall, but definitely the disciplinarian of the family. He seemed to always know what the children were up to and never hesitated to correct their behavior but the children did not live in fear of their father. The children were encouraged to participate in conversations, and were respected as valued family members. The elders took the time to converse with the children. Alexei had a strong sense of family and security in his peaceful home.

Alexei's mother, Ayironga, was his main caretaker. His mother nursed him until about the age of four, and Alexei recalls being very upset that her milk had dried up after a week-long visit to see her parents. She was always patient, kind and protective, and she loved to sing as she worked. One of her favorite songs was about a slave trader named Patricio who took all of the able-bodied men from the village, causing the crops to fade and die from inattention.

Alexei's mother was also responsible for making the "wine" that more resembled gin, brewed from grains of sorghum, corn and millet with sweet potato added for sweetness. Alexei recalls watching her dry out the millet, then grinding and mashing the grain in water before leaving it to soak. Sorghum was used as the fermenting agent, taking a few days to begin gurgling. On the fourth day, the mash was ready to boil and the vapor would be collected inside a tube to condense and run into a pan as it cooled. The wine was used for celebrations and as a reward for hard work during the harvest season. The Acholi people did not consume alcohol daily. Unlike the city, the rural village areas had no regulations regarding the production or sale of alcohol.

Life in Alexei's village was fairly predictable, since it revolved around the farming and hunting. Alexei recalls the air always smelling fresh. During the rainy season the air had the moist smell of dew - very clean. In the dry season Alexei remembers the pungent smell of burning vegetation created by farmers clearing their crops to make way for the next planting. Alexei lived at home in the village until he graduated sixth grade.

Boarding School
In Uganda, it was customary for children to attend boarding school beginning with grade seven. Alexei was accepted at St. Joe's Secondary School, about seventy miles south of Akara. One of his brothers owned a store in the area, so Alexei spent most of his vacations at his brother's house. The transition from life at home to boarding school seemed very easy to Alexei. Education had always been encouraged and much was expected of him. He always earned one of the top three grades in his school and qualified for government scholarships, which paid for his tuition, room and

board, with a small stipend left over. Of course his family was proud and encouraged him to make the most of the opportunity, even though it meant being separated from their baby.

In high school Alexei moved to St. Leo's, a boarding school run by a group of Americans called The Holy Cross Brothers. It was located in west Uganda near the border of Zaire, and next to an active volcano by the name of Mt. Rwenzori. Alexei remembers a violent earthquake in the tenth grade that shook the school. The students, fearful that the building would collapse, slept outside for the next week.

After graduating the twelfth grade, Alexei studied accounting at a junior college for three years. The only options for higher education were the junior college and the university. The common perception was that those attending university were "do-nothings" whereas students who attended junior college were prepared for careers in the real world. Upon graduation, Alexei accepted his first job at the central bank in Kampala. Alexei found the position tedious, as it dealt primarily with retail and commercial bank regulations, and offered no chance for human interaction, so Alexei didn't stay there long. His next position was at Grindlays Bank, a British commercial bank that provided him with extensive training in all aspects of the banking business. As an accounting graduate, Alexei qualified for a supervisory position. Alexei remained at Grindlays until the Idi "Daddy" Amin coup.

Amin

Amin's coup was devised as a strategy to avoid arrest and prosecution for the assassination of his boss, Brigadier Pierino Okoya, deputy chief of the army. One of his first actions after seizing power from President Milton Obote was to force out all foreign-run businesses from Uganda. The financial institutions were either taken over by Amin's local national bank or they folded. This included Grindlays Bank where Alexei worked. Another major action brought about by Amin's regime was the takeover by locals of all commercial economic activities previously owned and operated by British, Indian and Pakistani merchants. Ugandans believed this was a good move. They had long felt resentment for the colonialists who operated and profited from most of the commerce.

Following their expulsion, the colonialists sabotaged the Ugandan economy by blocking trade conducted by the locals. New machinery parts could not be located and other necessities were blocked by the colonialists ejected from Uganda's economy. These actions prompted Amin to turn to the Arab world for assistance. Amin was from the Sudan and was a staunch Moslem who made it clear that anyone desiring to succeed to an influential position in his regime must convert to Islam. The Arab countries providing aid expected to see conversions.

The new regime caused immediate disruption in the cities and urban areas, and it was not long before the citizens in the rural towns and villages began to see major changes. Farmers were encouraged to form cooperatives in order to sell their crops for cash. Although they had to pay more to belong, they were now part-owners with a voice in the decision-making process. This was perceived by the farmers to be a positive change.

Immediately following the assassination of Okoya, an Acholi tribesman, Amin set forth the tide of violence through ruthless tactics. Because many of the armed forces were Acholi, Amin ordered them murdered in their barracks. From there on, the Acholi tribe was branded enemy number one, as Amin feared revenge. Any member of the Acholi tribe who was believed to be in a position of power or influence was marked for death. Amin's strategy was to dispatch squads to roam the city and countryside in search of members of the Acholi tribe. They were ambushed, kidnapped and killed, with assistance from informants in neighboring tribes who reported their neighbors and co-workers out of envy.

Alexei's uncles were in the first group of soldiers slaughtered by Amin's death squads. Alexei's older brother had been working as a mechanic on the amphibious fleet, and Amin retained him as he was fascinated by exotic amphibious cars. Alexei's brother soon went into hiding, knowing that his survival had only been a result of winning Amin's capricious favor. Alexei's sister was not as fortunate. She and her family were massacred by Amin's roaming death squads.

The Acholi tribe comprised about twenty percent of the Ugandan population. The Baganda tribe was the largest, residing primarily in central and southern Kampala, close to Lake Victoria. The Banyakole tribe lived in southern Uganda and the Batoro and Bunyoro tribes in the southwest. To the east were the Bagisu, the Iteso and the Langi tribes. The Langi tribe also suffered persecution at the hands of Amin.

Alexei was forced into hiding after Amin's soldiers came to his place of work, and then to his home, searching for him. He hid in the bush lands for more than one week. It was the beginning of 1977. Amin ordered the execution of Archbishop Luwum, an Acholi tribesman and an outspoken critic of Amin's reign of terror and violence. That same year, the death squads escalated their activities. Alexei could see no end to the massacres and persecution, and realized that he had to flee the country for good. His decision left him conflicted, since it meant leaving his family, including four children, and his position at the bank. There was really no other option than to leave, or stay and be hunted down.

Friends helped Alexei to obtain a transfer to a remote bank in a small, one-road town. The narrow road scaled the mountains, curving with perilous turns. Alexei made it to the town, Kapeharwa, and waited until he could be smuggled across to Kenya. Alexei could not have turned back, even if he had wanted to, as Amin's soldiers had taken up a post guarding the only road. When it was time, Alexei, dressed as the tractor mechanic for a Department of Agriculture researcher, crossed the border on foot. He was dressed in government supply overalls, and was supposedly coming to town to collect supplies which the researcher would come to pick up.

Kenya

Once in Kenya, Alexei boarded a bus bound for Nairobi. Having made his way to the United Nations High Commission for Refugees, he promptly registered himself. He was given temporary housing and a small stipend for food. Alexei spent one and a half years in Kenya, unable to work. The Kenyan government had banned the hiring of Ugandan refugees, fearing destabilization of the labor force in Kenya. The only positions they were allowed to accept were in education. Alexei visited the United Nations Commission daily to glean whatever new information might be available about opportunities to migrate.

During one visit, Alexei met a professor from the University of Kenya who was from Alexei's hometown. He offered Alexei support, advice and encouragement. He encouraged Alexei to attend classes since he was not permitted to work. Soon Alexei was provided with news about scholarships available in the United States for those with excellent academic scores and experience in a relevant field. Alexei applied and was invited to accept a full scholarship at the community college in Denver, Colorado. The paperwork was processed by the United Nations, which took about a month. Alexei finally had his traveling documents!

For six months after Alexei fled from Uganda, his family did not know if he had survived or not. They only knew that he had disappeared, as had thousands of others before him. Human rights groups estimate Amin and his death squads slaughtered between 100,000 and 500,000 people during his eight years in power.

Amin was ousted by a group comprised of Acholi and Langi tribal members who had fled to Tanzania immediately after the coup, along with the Tanzanian government and the former president, Milton Obote. Obote had spent the eight years in exile in Tanzania, helping them to organize his return to power. Eventually Milton Obote was reinstalled to his position as president, and Amin fled to Saudi Arabia. Although the majority of the violence ended, the persecution of Acholi tribesmen continued. Obote is of the Baganda tribe, who at one time had been herdsmen for the Acholi.

These inequalities in social status were still remembered and punished. When asked about his most difficult experience, Alexei says that it was being a stranger in Kenya. Knowing no one, unable to speak the language, unable to qualify for work, and not knowing where his next meal would come from was all very traumatic. Alexei was much better equipped to survive hiding in the bush and living off the land. As a refugee, Alexei found himself stripped of all his tools and survival skills. His education, which he had earned through determination and dedication, meant nothing in this new foreign land. He and his fellow Ugandans were not wanted. They were seen as a threat to the Kenyan economy and work force.

United States
Once Alexei made it to the United States, he found himself searching for answers. He enrolled in Economics courses in the hopes of finding the answers to questions like, "What makes the world tick?" He read voraciously in the same quest. Finally, he discovered the answer: "Greed and the pursuit of power at all costs are what make the world tick." This was especially true in countries like Uganda, which fell victim to slave traders, colonialists, and merciless rulers. Alexei knew he wanted to steer clear of societies and institutions that embraced these doctrines.

Alexei's arrival to the US was sponsored through the Episcopal Church. He and a friend arrived in 1978, living in a commune of sorts with the priest and the priest's family. The religion, while based on many of the same doctrines as the Catholic Church, was very foreign to Alexei. He couldn't understand why they would live segregated from the rest of the community. Alexei and his friend were the only people of color in the commune. Later he learned that black people had a church of their own and did not mix. This was an odd concept for Alexei. The commune demanded rigorous attention to prayer, worshipping several times daily and all day on Sunday. Alexei began to feel caged, wishing to interact with the community at large.

Alexei discussed this wish with the priest, and both agreed that it would be best if Alexei and his friend found an apartment in Denver. Alexei began to work for the University of Denver to support himself while continuing with his studies. His first year in the commune had been very hard and he found a wide divide between his faith as a practicing Catholic in Uganda and the devotion he saw practiced in the commune. He realized that religion in the United States included strong elements of business, and was used as a way to make a living rather than operating purely out of the pursuit of faith.

The church and the missionaries in Uganda were there to improve the standards of living and provide education to the country's children. Alexei did not see the same priorities in the United States' Episcopal Church. Alexei had served as an altar boy in the Catholic Church for nine years in Uganda. He knew the mass backwards and forwards. Alexei relished hearing the mass recited in Latin, as it carried a mysticism which does not translate to any other language without distorting the meaning. He still longs for the spiritual nurturing of his soul through the Latin mass.

At times, Alexei wonders how he ended up in San Diego, working among the underserved in the "concrete jungle" of City Heights. Alexei does not believe in coincidences, but has faith that destiny has led him through his life experiences to education, health and community service. When Alexei was in the seventh and eighth grades, he volunteered in the school's dispensary. This provided him with an orientation to basic health care services. After immigrating to the United States, he worked in the Denver Medical Library for years. Through his interaction with doctors and scientists there, Alexei learned an extensive amount of medical information. It was during this time that Alexei met and married the daughter of a physician. In keeping with his trust in destiny, Alexei was moved to become a volunteer board member for a community health center, La Maestra Community Health Centers, in City Heights.

Returning Home
In 1982, after graduating with a BA in Economics, Alexei returned to Uganda to visit his parents and family. He took his professor from the University of Colorado along with him. The political unrest had settled down and he was finally able to travel freely throughout the country. This was the last time that Alexei would see his parents alive.

After hearing of the death of his parents, Alexei returned again to Uganda in 1999 to conduct final funeral rites for his parents. He was not able to go into Akara, the Acholi village of his childhood, due to a rebel insurgency against the current government. Alexei was happy to visit with his four children, now grown to adulthood with families of their own. Alexei still hopes for the day he can provide his parents with a proper burial, in keeping with their customs.

When Alexei was told of his mother's death, he went in to a state of shock. She had died the previous October, but he did not receive the news until April. At the time, Alexei was living in Colorado. He desperately wanted to return his homeland, but could not. Alexei became depressed and angry at the world, a world that had divided him from his family and kept them separated for so many years. He decided to take a leave from the University of Colorado and visit a Ugandan friend living in San Diego. It was during this visit that he decided to relocate his family to San Diego.

San Diego

San Diego reminded Alexei of his homeland in many ways. There were many more African refugees in San Diego than in Denver, and that comforted him. As he met refugee families and heard their stories, he was able to draw on the similarities to his own experiences. It was this commonality that attracted him to the community of City Heights. Alexei felt drawn, as if by a magnet, to helping others find their way in this new land of opportunity. In his quest to work in community development, Alexei created the framework for an organization which would provide assistance and support to refugee families seeking healthcare, housing and jobs.

To Alexei's dismay, he encountered some of the same disruptive forces, fueled by the greed and thirst for power, in the so-called leaders of San Diego's African community. The realization was a shock to Alexei. He had assumed that in this new country, there could not possibly be people who would want to take advantage of their fellow countrymen and refugees, for the sole purpose of elevating themselves into positions of power and leadership. It was this rude awakening that compelled Alexei to devote his time to correcting the imbalance, to become involved with organizations that would truly develop the underserved communities of San Diego. To support his household, Alexei became a realtor. This allowed him time to devote to his true passion of helping others.

Most people who know Alexei would describe him as easygoing and very sociable, yet extremely tenacious. Since arriving in San Diego, Alexei has worked for various community-based organizations and served on numerous non-profit boards and committees. He continues to advocate for the underserved, and is most recently director for the Housing and Community Development Center, a non-profit organization in City Heights.

Alexei maintains a strong network of fellow expatriates, former colleagues and friends. He is forever tracking them down, never failing to meet with one or two when he is traveling through their "neck of the jungle". One long-time friend is the current treasurer for Papua New Guinea; another is the governor of Belize; and still another works for the Denver City Planning Department. All live totally different lives, but share a common past.

Alexei plans to continue his work in community development in San Diego, but hopes that, one day, he can use his considerable network to help in the rebuilding of his native country. Alexei has one daughter and two sons in the United States, and holds on to the dream that sometime in the not-too-distant future, he will take them to visit Uganda, to see and experience the land of their father's roots.

QUESTIONS

1. What was the structure of the village where Alexei grew up?

2. What was the family structure?

3. Was there a belief a higher power/being?

4. What educational opportunities were available?

5. Who provided the education? (i.e. government, religious institutions, etc.)

6. Was education available for all?

7. How does this differ from educational opportunities in the US?

8. Describe the tribes and their influence on society.

9. Are there any commonalities between the tribal structures and society in the US?

10. How did villagers make their living?

11. What celebrations existed to mark life events held special by this culture?

12. What were some of the specific customs?

13. Are there any similarities between the customs in Alexei's village and in the US today? How do they differ?

14. How did the political events in Alexei's experience affect society? What changes occurred? Were they dramatic, life-changing effects?

15. Were there any influences or support outside of Uganda which fueled the violence and political upheaval?

16. What happened to the societal structure when the new governmental regime took power?

17. How did this affect the farmers? Was this a positive change for the farmers in the long run?

18. What was Amin's strategy to gain control of the government and country?

19. Can you imagine facing similar upheavals in the US? (i.e., a major political upheaval which changes life as you know it; World War; Outside investors taking control of the USA; the fall of our government supported by outside forces and funds,…)

20. What events led Alexei to flee his country? What options did he have?

21. Can you identify with any of the trauma he must have experienced in leaving his family, work, career, and finding himself at a survival level, with a very uncertain future?

22. Once in Kenya, was Alexei welcomed? How did the attitude of some Kenyans compare with how some Americans view immigrants?

23. What were some of the challenges he faced there?

24. Where did Alexei's strength and determination to survive come from?

25. What were some of the thoughts and feelings that Alexei experienced upon his arrival to the USA?

26. What pre-conceived ideas and hopes do you think he had about his new country? Were they realistic?

27. What marketable skills did Alexei arrive with to the USA in order for him to find employment and mainstream into society?

28. What societal values and customs from Alexei's past helped him to fit into mainstream America?

29. Did Alexei eventually find a city in the US where he felt at home?

30. What challenges did Alexei see existing in the refugee populations in San Diego?

31. Has Alexei made the transition from survivor to thriver? If so, what are some of the indications?

32. What strikes you as significant in this real life story?

33. Why do you think Alexei chose the line of work he did and still does in San Diego?

34. What were his other options?

35. Has Alexei adopted this country as his own?

36. Do you consider Alexei to be an American?

37. What strengths does Alexei bring to this country and to our society?

38. What interested you most about this story? What will you take away from this story?

39. Do you know anyone like Alexei?

40. What responsibilities and roles do we as the host country need to provide to people who are brought here, like Alexei?

41. What can you do to help refugees settle into their new country?

42. Regardless of how or why the refugees are here, what solutions can we come up with to facilitate their mainstreaming into our society?

Ali's Story

My name is Abdulkadir Mohamed Ali, or "Ali", and I am an American. I came from Somalia as a refugee when I was seventeen years old on October 27, 1993. My mother was the first one of my family to arrive in the United States in 1992 through the IRC (International Rescue Committee). She then petitioned for me and my sister. There were five of us boys and four sisters. Three have died. Before coming to the United States, I lived in the Otanga refugee camp in Mombasa, near Nairobi, for two years. It was a very long two years.

Mogadishu
My family operated stores in Mogadishu, the capital of Somalia. That's where I was born, the youngest of nine children. Life seemed peaceful to me, and my family was all together. My father was a businessman who ran stores and mini markets. He loved to talk to people at the local coffee shop where they sold coffee, tea, cakes and *sambusas*. He died of a heart attack in 1983, so my mother and brothers took over the businesses.

Civil War
The civil war started in Somalia in 1990. There hasn't been peace ever since.

The military government led by dictator Mohamed Siad Barre had been in power for twenty-one years, and was supported by the governments of Russia and Cuba and by Saddam Hussein of Iraq. Somalia has lots of untapped oil. It is also rich in gold, fish and bananas. All businesses had to have permission from the government to operate, import or export; otherwise, the government would confiscate everything.

The people wanted to drive out the military from their ruling position and have the freedom to change the president and the government. Civil unrest built up, finally leading to the civil war. Forces led by General Mohamed Farrah Aidid took Mogadishu in 1991. However, at the same time the Somali National Movement declared independence for Somaliland in the northwest with a new president, a new flag, a new government. Puntland in the northeast also broke away. These two regions are still fighting today.

All of our lives were turned upside down. When the civil war began, my uncles were put in jail because they spoke out against the government, advocating for freedom. All of our businesses and properties were confiscated. I was in Mogadishu at the time and witnessed the takeover of the city. They began looting property, raping women and girls and killing hundreds of people.

Otanga Refugee Camp
In 1992, the United States arrived with the United Nations through Ethiopia to stop the violence, starvation and killing and to bring freedom. A lot of people had to escape. I fled by bus to the border with Kenya. It took me seven days to get there, without sufficient food or water. When I arrived, the Kenyan government put me in a jail cell, where I stayed for two months. Luckily, the United Nations gave me a tent, blanket and food after I was released from the cell.

I was sent, along with my sister, to the Otanga refugee camp in Kenya. There were 120,000 refugees living there. We lived there for two years and don't know how we survived. Thousands died from malaria, tuberculosis and parasites. Currently, there are 200,000 refugees there.

There was one medical clinic in the camp with twenty part-time doctors. The wait time to see a doctor was very long and they had some medicine there but not enough. Water was imported for all of the refugees by tanks and was strictly rationed. The guards in the camp were Kenyan. They were very bad. They whipped and beat the refugees regularly. It was clear that they did not like us and they wanted more money to take care of the refugees. The women and girls in the camp were raped by the Kenyan military, despite the intervention from the United Nations who told them to stop.

Life was horrible for me and everyone there. I escaped once but I was captured and sent back. I stayed there for one more month until I was granted an interview with the United States embassy. My mother had already submitted the petitions to sponsor me and my sister, which was how I was able to come to the United States. The immigration documents and all official documents in the United States require birthdates, which we did not have records of. In our culture, we do not celebrate our birth date, as it is not important. We consider religious holidays to be special and only those dates are celebrated. So a lot of Somalis have chosen January 1st as their birth date. It is confusing to Americans. This was a challenge for us and still is.

San Diego

When I came to the City Heights area of San Diego in 1993, I wanted to finish my high school. However, I was already seventeen years old and could not attend the local school, Hoover High. I started driving a taxi and could sometimes earn two hundred dollars a night. It was a thriving business back then. Now the taxi drivers earn twenty dollars a night because of the depressed economy; tourism is down and less people are traveling.

I suffered for years from ear complications resulting from bombings back in Somalia. I have had three ear operations in the United States and now I am a lot better. I am really grateful for that, as my ears bothered me a lot. The pressure in the ears caused me to hear roaring and they hurt a lot.

The Somali community in San Diego is now very large. Thousands of refugees were settled here and thousands of others have come from Minnesota, where they were originally resettled. The weather here is more similar to Somalia's and we have already formed community organizations to help the people. Ninety-eight percent of Somalis are Moslem. We are a very peaceful and connected community. We have faced many challenges in San Diego.

Housing has been a challenge. Through the resettlement agencies we were placed in low-income housing, mostly rundown apartments in very rough neighborhoods. The Somali community worked with the San Diego Police Department to move into gang and drug-infested neighborhoods to bring stability to the areas. There were two public housing projects where more than twenty Somali families were asked to move in to stabilize the area. Of course there were many repercussions. Many Somali were attacked, beaten and robbed at the beginning. Eventually, the criminals were pushed out. There is still some violence, but we deal with it.

The San Diego Police Department hired members of the Somali community to act as liaisons and have helped us achieve success. They also educated us on our rights as citizens and that the police were not our enemy. Back in Somalia, we were fearful of the police as they were part of the military government who were not there to protect us. We were afraid to call for help because we thought that the police were like back in Somalia. The criminals knew that we as refugees here would not call the police, so they had the freedom to torment us constantly without any recourse. We have learned that when a crime occurs, it is okay to call the police. Now we feel a lot safer.

It has been difficult to acculturate, as our culture is so different. Back in Somalia, we were brought up to obey and follow what our elders said. They were very respected. Here in America, our elders do not speak the language and have to get used to new ways of living. We have to take care of our old people and they are not independent. Also, the teenagers see their peers who are different and are attracted to new lifestyles. I have to realize that my children are American and will grow up differently than I did.

Somali people have many children. According to our religion, it is a blessing to have many children. In America, both the husband and wife must work, so it is hard to make sure that our children are safe. My wife and I are struggling to help them take advantage of the opportunities for education and jobs that are available in this new country. We are afraid for our children. They are not free to walk around the neighborhoods, and even at school there are gangs that attack them because they are different. The Somali community has organized religious school for the children on the weekends so they can learn about the Koran and have activities that are safe. Still, we are afraid for them and want them to be safe.

I have noticed that many Americans are suspicious of Moslems. The Somali population in the United States really suffered when the 9/11 tragedy occurred. Our community issued a press release stating that the Somali community was very upset about what occurred and does not participate in any terrorist activity or any actions that would harm our new country. We said that our religion does not support killings of any kind. In fact, the Koran has the same core commandments as the Bible. Unfortunately, the terrorists were Moslem, though of a different sect. Most people do not understand that difference, so they group us all as Moslems together, assuming that we Somalis agree with the terrorists. That is not true at all. We suffered so much in Somalia and then in the refugee camps. The last thing we want is trouble in our new country, a country that has given us freedom and offered us many opportunities.

It was very difficult to find healthcare providers that could understand Somali culture and communicate with us. That is why we value La Maestra Community Health Centers so much. They opened their doors to us, welcomed us, and even hired and trained many from the Somali community to make the services culturally competent, which really improved the health conditions. La Maestra's job training and placement program gave many of us the skills we needed to find work in many places. Through La Maestra's network, we were placed in other community-based organizations like schools, preschools, pharmacies, laboratories and others. These programs are what we needed to adapt to this society and get a good start.

Helping People Find their Way

I chose to come to work at La Maestra Community Health Centers on February 10, 2006. I had been a patient for years, as had my wife. Our eight children were all delivered by the doctors from La Maestra. So I knew the organization well and saw how many needy people they help with medical, dental, mental health services, social services and job training. I want to help my community, the Somali community, and all other cultures. I feel very good being part of an organization that helps people when they do not know where to turn. I see so many people who are refugees and immigrants that are totally lost. My job is to help them with transportation so they know where to go for their healthcare and social services. Then, they learn the way and can get there themselves. I also translate a lot and show them where to go for housing and jobs. It is very rewarding for me to help people to transition from being lost, to finding a resource like La Maestra and, eventually, getting jobs and building a good life and future for their families. I give them encouragement.

I voted for the first time as an American citizen in November of 2008. I am proud to be an American.

My wife and I are very excited about our children's future in the United States. They have opportunities to become educated, obtain scholarships, and choose what profession or trade they want to pursue. I see my oldest daughter so proficient on the computer already and wanting to become a court reporter. That is her dream. We encourage our children to study hard and be good people, respect God and others.

QUESTIONS

1. Where is Ali from?

2. How did Ali's family support themselves there? What socioeconomic class was Ali's family from?

3. In what year did the Civil War in Somalia begin? Why did it occur?

4. How did this affect Ali's family? What are some of the atrocities Ali and his community faced during the war?

5. How did Ali escape from Somalia?

6. Where did Ali travel to? What happened when he arrived?

7. Which refugee camp did he go to? How many people lived in the camp? How long did he stay there?

8. What were some of the illnesses in the camp? Were there enough medical doctors and medicine?

9. Was there enough food water for the refugees in the camp?

10. Who were the guards in the camp? How did they treat the refugees?

11. Were the women and girls respected by the guards?

12. What happened when Ali tried to escape from the camp?

13. How did Ali get to come to the US?

14. Why were birthdates a problem for the Somali?

15. How old was Ali when he came to San Diego? Was he able to attend school?

16. What kind of work did Ali find?

17. What health problem does Ali suffer from? Why does he have this problem?

18. Where did most of the Somali refugees in the US settle? Why?

19. What challenges does the Somali community face in San Diego?

20. What repercussions did the Somali face in the neighborhoods where they were settled?

21. How have the Somali refugees helped to stabilize these violent neighborhoods? Have the police collaborated with them?

22. Why were the Somali afraid of the police when they first arrived to the US?

23. What are some of the issues the Somali community faces in the US?

24. What are some of the major differences between Somali and American culture, according to Ali?

25. Why do Somali families have many children?

26. What fears do Ali and his wife have for their children in the US? What opportunities do they see for their children?

27. How did the Somali community feel about the 9/11 tragedy?

28. How do the Somali feel about the terrorists who are Moslem?

29. Why do the Somali feel grateful to the US?

30. Why was it difficult for the Somali community to access healthcare in San Diego? Have the Somali found a medical home in San Diego?

31. What opportunities did La Maestra Community Health Centers offer to the Somali community?

32. How did Ali find his current employment? Why does he feel proud of the work he is doing?

33. Is Ali a United States citizen?

34. What future do Ali and family look forward to in the US?

ALICIA'S STORY

"When I was little, I would watch my mother as she mended my father's already patched work shirt. Each time she did it, she would say that she didn't know how she would be able to do it, sewing patches on top of patches. Right then, I made the decision that when I grew up, I would buy my father new clothes. And I did!"

Michoacán
Alicia Pimentel Rodríguez was born February 15, 1940 in Pátzcuaro, Michoacán, Mexico. She was one of five children, until the deaths of her ten-year-old sister Elena and her six-year-old brother Luis, both in the same year. Before Luis's untimely death, he was often found crying in the graveyard, calling out to his recently deceased sister, "Nena!" It was said that little Luis died of grief. That left three girls, Martha, Alicia and Cella.

Alicia's father, José Campos, was born in 1905 in Purepero, Michoacán. When he was only a small child, José's father abandoned his family to move to the United States. During the war, José's mother died of typhoid fever. Because the nurses at the small hospital could not bring themselves to tell the child that his mother was dead, they allowed José to return day after day to inquire about her recovery. After the news of her death was finally shared, José wandered the streets, aimless and depressed, and without a family to take him in. He taught himself to read, and when he was twelve years old, he found an ad placed by his father in the newspaper's classifieds section. His father had been searching for him and had included an address in Los Angeles, California. Having survived alone on the streets, José had no fear of jumping trains and hitching rides to make his way to his father. Upon arrival, his father was overwhelmed with joy at the reunion, having given up all hope of finding his son.

José spent the next several years in Los Angeles working in construction and married an American woman. José was considered an attractive man, of slender, medium build with pale skin and light brown eyes. One day, José returned home unexpectedly to find his wife in bed with another man.

The two men fought and, before it was over, his wife's lover fell from the balcony to his death. José was arrested, tried for manslaughter and sent to prison. After his release, José returned to his native land to leave the tragedy behind and start a new life. It was there that he met and married Alicia's mother. José's father remained in Los Angeles until he was old and sick, and only then did he allow José to take him back to Mexico where the family cared for him until his death.

José never got over the sadness of his mother's loss, or his time as an orphan in the streets. He suffered from bouts of stomach pain which sometimes prevented him from working for long stretches of time. Alicia's mother would do her part, taking in washing and ironing, but it was not enough to keep the family fed.

Alicia's mother, Maria Rodríguez Campos, was born in 1908 in the little Michoacán town of San Juan Tumbio. Maria had one sister and one brother. Maria's mother was a member of the Purepecha tribe of Indians. When Maria was three years old, her mother died. Maria and her siblings moved from the tribe they knew to live in a small hut with their father. Sometimes Maria's father would leave the children by themselves for days at a time, leaving a log burning in the grate for warmth, and little else. The children scavenged for nuts, pears and peaches. The closest neighbors lived far away, but would sometimes bring the children in to feed them.

When Maria was five years old, an aunt came and took both girls to her home in Pátzcuaro. Maria's eighteen-year-old brother died shortly thereafter. When Maria was seven, she started working with a priest's sister. With her first paycheck she bought a *rebozo*, a large cotton shawl, to cover her single set of clothes. When the priest moved to Mexico City, Maria's sister Gabina accompanied him, hoping to find work so she could send money back for Maria's care. She was able to send money for awhile, but soon Gabina disappeared and was never heard from again. Maria continued to work, living with her aunt, until the time she met José and they married.

When Alicia was four years old, her father moved his family to the nearby city of Uruapan, Michoacán, where a relative had helped him to secure a construction job. Alicia and her father José moved in advance of the rest of the family, staying with his friend Amalia. Amalia had a son named Ezequiel, who was around Alicia's age. He resented Alicia's intrusion, and would frequently torment her. It was rumored that the boy was actually her half-brother, son to her father and Amalia. After some time, José built a one room adobe house with a thatched roof. Inside was a small kitchen with a wood burning stove. Water was more than a half mile away and had to be hand-carried from the stream to the house. Alicia remembers the house being very cold without an enclosed roof. In fact, when Alicia was older, she would climb up onto the lattice covering the house and pour water down onto her sisters, to stop their incessant arguing.

José's faith in God was strong, and he was a staunch believer in the traditional family unit. José was a strict parent, and never permitted his daughters to have boyfriends, or men of any kind inside their home. The oldest daughter Martha eloped at a very young age, marrying the son of a nearby rancher. The family had called on José to formally request Martha's hand in marriage, but José had adamantly refused. So Martha gathered her few belongings and jumped out of the window to join her husband-to-be and his family. They wed immediately. Martha escaped what she believed to be an overly strict and impoverished home, only to end up in an equally confining situation. She worked hard for the rest of her life, bearing ten children to her rancher husband. Alicia had other plans.

When she was six, Alicia traveled through the neighborhood, offering to do small jobs. Because of her age, she was not always taken seriously. Alicia's winning personality and positive attitude finally won over one neighbor, who employed Alicia to help take care of her numerous children. In addition to the few *pesos* she would earn, the neighbor would give her leftover food to bring home to her family. Each day on her way to work, Alicia would look up to the sky and speak to God. She would tell him that if she could find a peso in the street, she would give twenty *centavos* to the church and buy tortillas and a chunk of cheese for her family with the rest. At first, she did not tell her parents that she was working, and they would ask where she was getting the food. Alicia would invent half-truths, always concocting a plausible reason for going out early each day. Of course, they were hardly in a position to object when she came home with fruit, beans and rice.

Alicia found another part-time job working at a fruit stand. She would take the orders, and then blend the fruit juice. The owner quickly noticed how efficient Alicia was at running the stand, collecting the money and making correct change. She would leave Alicia in charge of the fruit stand for hours at a time and Alicia remembers the thrill of running the small business. Little Alicia was completely comfortable interacting with customers, making jokes and always went about her work with a positive attitude. Alicia was delighted to take home the leftover fruit, as well as the tips left by customers. One of her family's favorite treats was fried bananas with *piloncillo* (brown unrefined sugar).

On the outskirts of the town was the small Purepecha indigenous community. The current president of Mexico, Felipe Calderón, is a descendent of the

Purepechas of Morelia, Michoacán. Alicia recalls attending their celebrations along with the other children, watching the beautiful Purepecha girls as they danced, dressed in vibrant colors, elaborately embroidered blouses, and skirts that they would swoosh from side to side. They wore their hair in two long braids, each side adorned with fresh flowers. The young men wore white shirts and pants, and big sombreros with red scarves around their necks. Alicia was fascinated by the embroidery on their clothing and would commit the patterns to memory so she could later replicate them onto blouses, tablecloths and veils.

Alicia especially enjoyed some of the Purepecha festival songs. One of her favorites was sung by the entire group singing in chorus:

Noparanguacho mi reinita, mi reinita
Noparacuichu
Juilla, isla cuanchbi
Aguachimba, mi reinito,
Ni jua nis carate aqui
Alla cuira ashancuin qui
Ten mucho cuidado con estos ojitos y con esta boquita

Then the girls would sign a refrain:
Cuacho, mucha chupiri uino

Then the boys would sing in response:
Caoicho pero no tondoco.

One of Alicia's favorite performances was the traditional *Danza de los Viejitos*, where dancers dressed like elderly men would dance slowly with canes and hunched over backs, and then suddenly break into upbeat, vigorous tap dance style moves. Alicia, always curious, would observe the festivities of the village to learn about the lives and customs of the Purepecha tribe. Special dishes were prepared, including *tamales* and *caldo de res*, a soup made with beef, bone marrow, tripe, corncob pieces, beans, squash, *nopales* (cactus), cabbage, salt, a leaf of *epazote* and three kinds of *chiles*. After a few hours, Alicia's father would come looking for her, worried that one of the Indians would take her away to his village to keep her for a wife. This was a common occurrence during the festivals.

Alicia remembers liking one of the little boys in her village. She told his grandmother that when she was older, she was going to marry him. The grandmother laughed and told her that before she could marry him, she would first have to complete her Holy Communion. Alicia promptly set about studying the Bible and taking catechism classes. Her shabby attire made her embarrassed to go to class. Up to this time, Alicia's mother had made her undergarments out of used flour sacks. Alicia set out to collect remnants of old clothing and began to sew, making up her own style of clothing. She continued with her classes, and as with everything else she tried, Alicia's efforts earned her first prize in the church.

As Alicia gained more and more confidence with her sewing abilities, she began to do mending for extra income, and laundry which she would wash by hand. She sewed blouses, embroidered, and made veils, using some of the same patterns she remembered from the festivals. She was patient at needlework. Her skill as a seamstress grew, and in a short time she began to design and sew clothes to sell in the village. She convinced her father to allow her to work outside the home as long as she continued with her lessons. She was already behind in her studies, since she had started elementary school late, but made up for the delay and graduated eighth grade with honors. Alicia enjoyed school and her memory for detail was excellent. The only part of school she did not enjoy was marching and dancing. It seemed that no matter how she tried, she could not coordinate herself well enough to move in tandem with the other students. Alicia knew that her parents could not afford to send her to secondary school, so she concentrated on supplementing her daily work with jobs sewing at home.

Alicia heard about a job in a factory established by then president Lázaro Cárdenas. She accepted a job washing, ironing and cooking for 100 pesos a week. She was very happy with the arrangement. Each night when she returned home from work, she would commence with her home jobs of washing, ironing and sewing. It was at about this time that Jóse's health started declining. Alicia remembers returning from work one day to find her father doubled over in pain. Up until this time, the family never had enough money to pay for a doctor. Alicia summoned the doctor, and paid for his services and medications from her meager savings. This helped for a time, until the next bout.

Alicia had many friends, and found that her vivaciousness attracted the boys. She was always careful not to be seen by her father in their company, as she knew he would forbid the interaction, even though José had always granted Alicia more freedom than he had her sisters. At age fifteen, Alicia received a formal marriage proposal which she considered seriously. As with her sister's proposal years earlier, her father was adamantly opposed. He advised her that she had considerably more potential and would have numerous opportunities for a good marriage. At first Alicia was strongly inclined to defy her father's refusal, but the words rang true in her heart. Alicia declined the offer and continued with her work and home business. Alicia enjoyed her freedom to create designs, build her home business and help support her family with her own earnings. She continued to thrive in this way for a few more years.

The Curandera

During one of her visits to an aunt in another city, Alicia met and fell in love with a young neighbor of her aunt. Alicia and the young man began to see each other often, and their relationship developed quickly. One day a woman stopped Alicia on the street to tell her that the young man with whom she was enchanted was married to another. This came as a complete shock to Alicia, and she set out to inquire of others to find the truth behind the statement. She accused the young man of being deceitful, but he swore it was not true. Alicia suddenly became physically ill, and nothing would alleviate her sickness. She left the city, and at the advice of her mother, went to stay with her sister Martha in the countryside to recuperate. It was there that her brother-in-law told her of a woman who could cure her, a well-known *curandera*, or healer.

Desperate to find a remedy and feel normal again, Alicia traveled with Martha and her husband to see the curandera. The woman took one look at Alicia and told her that she was suffering from an evil spell. She gathered some herbs and immediately started cleansing treatments. At the end of the treatments, the curandera picked up an egg and passed it over Alicia. She instructed Alicia to hold the egg in her left hand, go to the sink and then break it open in a cup to see the originator of the spell. Alicia did as she was instructed. To her surprise, inside the egg was the image of the woman who had told her the lies about her young man. Alicia was stunned. The curandera sent her home with a strong warning not to accept a gift of food, specifically a dish of mole and rice, which would be delivered to her house the day after her return. Sure enough, the following day, a knock came at the door. Alicia opened the door to discover a child standing on her doorstep with a bowl of food. The child introduced herself as the daughter of the woman from the street, continuing on to say that her mother was aware that Alicia was ill and wanted to send her home some food. Alicia thanked the child, promptly throwing the dish away with her left hand, just as the curandera had instructed. Alicia was amazed at the curandera's clarity at prediction, and convinced herself to keep clear of the young man to avoid any further curse from the jealous woman. Alicia believed that the woman would go to any extreme to interfere with their future happiness. Alicia proceeded to break off the relationship for good, and made a miraculous recovery, her vivaciousness and positive spirit restored. This experience left Alicia with a strong respect for curanderas, and the power of evil intentions.

Tijuana

As time went on, José's childhood experiences continued to haunt him, his depression regained its hold and he began to drink heavily. The drinking continued for years and years. Alicia's sister Cella married and left the home. Alicia saw her ability to earn better wages challenged by the limitations of living in a small town. She knew that she would be unable to continue to support her parents, especially with her father's ill health and alcoholism, on her limited earnings. For his own part, José could no longer compete with the younger, stronger men for construction jobs. Both sisters, too, had financial difficulties. Alicia began to understand that her family's survival depended upon her. The cost of living was on the rise and no matter how much Alicia worked, she could not keep up with expenses. It was during this time that José's sister contacted the family and suggested they send Alicia to help her in Tijuana. Alicia convinced her father to let her go for a visit, to experience some new surroundings, and to see more of the world. Alicia's father and mother were hesitant to let her go, as if they had a premonition that Alicia would be gone for a very long time.

Alicia was preparing for her journey to visit her Aunt Lupe in Tijuana when her cousin Mari stopped by, asking if she could go along. So Alicia and Mari started off on their first big adventure. They traveled by bus for three days. When they arrived in Tijuana, they started looking for their aunt's house. They wandered around and around, finally stopping at a small store to ask the shopkeeper for directions. The lady was kind and invited the girls to have a seat while she called their aunt.

Alicia and Mari were astounded by the poverty that surrounded them. They had assumed that their aunt lived in better conditions. The walls of Lupe's house were riddled with holes, and it was very cold. At least there was food - handmade tortillas and beans. Alicia had a strong headache from the fatigue of her trip and a lack of food on the way. Mari had a sore throat and fever. The girls were feeling overwhelmed by their new situation, and weren't sure what they had left home for.

One day, they took a trip to the beach where neighbors gathered shells and mussels from beneath the rocks. They boiled them in a large pot, and ate them with *chile*. Neither Alicia nor Mari had ever tried shellfish, and although they found it disgusting, their hunger won over their revulsion. One of the neighbors asked if Alicia or Mari would come over to help, as her hired hand was sick and unable to work. Alicia jumped at the opportunity, especially since she knew the neighbor had electricity and heat. Alicia then convinced the neighbor to hire Mari on, as well. They worked hard and were paid $5 a day for cooking and cleaning for the people on a ranch.

It was there that they met another cousin, one of Aunt Lupe's children, who suggested they go to San Diego, California. He told them that the jobs were plentiful and the pay was much better than they could make in Mexico. He told them that all they needed to do to get across the border was to go under a wire fence. The girls talked it over. Their prospects in Tijuana were dismal, and it was decided that Alicia would take the chance. After all, their cousin had made is sound so easy.

San Diego

The cousin rounded up Alicia, along with some others, and left them standing at the border near the Tijuana airport. One person in the group instructed them to crawl through a long tube that was suspended over a deep canyon. They scooted through the seemingly endless tube, and Alicia remembers praying the whole time, terrified that they would drop into the canyon below and die. Finally they emerged from the tube, only to see bulls staring back at them. They were sure the bulls would gore them through, but instead they passed right by. By this time, it was 5:00 a.m. and they saw a ranch in the distance. Alicia and her group watched from the bushes as the INS agents drove by but luckily didn't see them hiding. A man in a truck appeared, picked them up and drove them to the house of one of Alicia's distant cousins.

Alicia found work doing odd jobs in a store. Although the pay was not good, Alicia stayed there for five months, not knowing what else to do. Alicia sent money to Mari in Tijuana to pay for her border crossing. Once she arrived, the girls went to stay with a friend in the Point Loma area of San Diego, where she was the housekeeper of a very spacious home. The friend, Doña Maria, instructed them to stay in her room because of the dogs on the estate and the alarms. The girls remained in the room for several days, quiet as mice, sometimes without food, terrified of venturing outside. Doña Maria found them housekeeping work near Moreno Boulevard and the girls were finally settled into this new land of opportunity.

Alicia and Mari learned that classes in English were being offered at Midway Adult School. As soon as class began, their instructor befriended them, inviting both girls to stay in her home in Mission Hills. They continued with their housekeeping jobs by day, returning home each night to the home in Mission Hills. The girls shared a room with the English teacher's two daughters, Zara, thirteen and Marina, just eighteen months. Their new friend was recently divorced, and was having a hard time with her ex-husband. Alicia and Mari were undaunted by this news, as they had already faced far greater challenges in recent months.

The new living arrangements were the beginning of a wonderful friendship between Alicia and Zara, one which would last more than thirty-five years. Although Alicia spoke no English and Zara spoke only English and a little Italian, that didn't stop the girls from communicating. They came from very different backgrounds and cultures, but had enough desire to communicate and befriend each another to overcome the obstacles. After two years Mari left, having gained employment as live-in domestic help for a wealthy family. She was a bit disappointed that Alicia stayed behind, clearly satisfied with her day job and her obligations in the teacher's home, helping with housework and care for Marina. Alicia also continued with her sewing, helping Zara to sew her own clothes. The family lacked funds to buy new clothes, but had enough to pay for fabric. Before long, Alicia had customers who wanted alterations and embroidery.

Five years after Alicia came to live with the teacher and her family, the teacher remarried and the situation in the household changed. After being part of the family for most of the time she had lived in San Diego, Alicia now had to find an apartment. She also took a position at a San Diego hotel. The work was demanding, but the tips were good. Alicia was responsible for cleaning and restocking the rooms on one hotel floor each day. The hotel manager expected perfection and timeliness, turning over each room at the specified interval. Alicia fell frequently, carrying the vacuum or cleaning products, always rushing to meet the quota. She would worry that the supervisor would find fault with her for not finishing the rooms on time.

Alicia realized that a lot of time was wasted running to retrieve the vacuum cleaner and the other cleaners needed for the job. All of the housekeepers had the same problem. During a staff meeting, the supervisor chided the housekeepers for not finishing the rooms more quickly. Alicia spoke up, suggesting that the management provide them with carts stocked with the cleaning products and vacuum. She explained that it would save a lot of time. The management listened, made the change, and the job ran much smoother. Then the supervisor added more rooms to each housekeeper's schedule. Alicia decided it was time to quit hotel work and return to cleaning private homes.

Alicia would get up at four o'clock each morning to catch the first in a series of buses that would carry her to her clients' neighborhoods. Sometimes the buses were late, and she would walk miles to catch the next connection. Every day was the same. Her clients appreciated her work, and were extremely satisfied with her attention to detail. Her positive attitude and flexibility kept her with a steady group of loyal clients. Alicia sent the majority of her earnings to her parents and siblings. She missed them dearly, but knew she could not chance visiting them and then have to face the border crossing again. On Sundays Alicia had a free day. She would go to church and then visit with family and friends. All of them were from Mexico, and had immigrated to the United States in search of a better life. They all sent money home to their families in Mexico. Each one encountered their own challenges, trying to survive in the new country without being picked up by INS and returned to Mexico. Some were luckier than others. Alicia's cheerful and gregarious personality continued to attract suitors, but she was hesitant to let anything distract her from her first responsibility to her family.

Aunt Alicia

One day Alicia's mother, Maria, wrote to tell her that her sister Cella's husband had disappeared, and that their children were living with her and Alicia's father. Cella had gone to Los Angeles to work, trying to save enough money to bring her husband and three children across. When news of her brother-in-law's disappearance reached Alicia, she became gravely concerned. Not long after, her father died and Alicia borrowed money to send for his funeral. That left Maria with three small children to provide for and take care of by herself. Alicia knew she had to do something, so she convinced her sister to allow Alicia to bring them across to San Diego. Alicia paid two hundred dollars for each child and five hundred dollars for her mother to be transported across the border. At the time, Alicia was living in a studio apartment in downtown San Diego. Alicia prayed that the crossing would be successful, and although she hadn't the first idea how they would manage once they got there, she knew there was no other option. The group made it as far as San Diego, where Cella had planned to meet them and take them to her home in Los Angeles. The only problem was that Cella kept getting picked up by INS and returned to Mexico. Once Cella made it back, she took her two youngest children to Los Angeles, leaving her oldest daughter and mother to live with Alicia.

Alicia, along with her mother and niece, moved into a dilapidated garage in the neighborhood of City Heights, where they made their home for the next ten years. The walls were infested with rats, opossums, cockroaches and termites. The nighttime activities in the alley next to the garage were terrifying - drug deals, fights and shootings were common occurrences. The rent was affordable for them, at three hundred fifty dollars a month, and most importantly, they were all together. Alicia continued to work, her niece attended school, and her mother stayed at home in the garage. They ventured out on Sundays, but were always back inside before nightfall. Alicia worried that her mother or niece might get sick and that she would have no way to pay for a doctor or healthcare services. When there was an illness, they relied on herbal teas and home remedies. Somehow they managed to survive.

Alicia raised her niece from the age of nine years old, while taking care of her mother until her death more than twenty years later. The family never received public assistance. Because Alicia worked using a borrowed social security number, she spent years paying taxes into a system with no hope of benefit. She accepted this willingly, since her family was surviving, and they placed their trust in God and her continued ability to support them.

When the Immigration Reform Act's Amnesty Program passed legislation in 1986, Alicia applied. She gained status as a legal resident, as did her sister and nieces and nephews. Once she became a citizen, the first thing she did was to apply on behalf of her mother. La Maestra Amnesty Center processed Maria's application, and it was granted. The relief for Alicia was indescribable. For the first time in more than 20 years, Alicia did not have to worry about her mother getting stopped and sent back to Mexico.

The family still had not applied for any public benefits. Her mother qualified for Medicare and had used it just one time. Maria had developed strong intestinal pains that would not go away. Alicia took her to a community clinic, and the clinic referred her to a gastrointestinal specialist. Maria waited weeks for the appointment to see the specialist. The pain became unbearable, so Alicia took her mother to the emergency room of a hospital in San Diego. The ER staff left her waiting on a cot for three hours before Alicia called the director of the clinic. The director went to the hospital and asked what was causing the delay. The hospital staff replied that because they did not have adequate proof of the patient's ability to pay, they were waiting to begin the tests and treatment until the payment could be guaranteed. It was only with the intervention of the clinic director that Maria's treatment began. How many other patients had a similar experience, one could only guess.

The on-call specialist at the hospital examined Maria, and advised the family that Maria had symptoms of advanced stomach cancer. They took her home and then back to Mexico, where Maria died and was buried. Preventive care would have made a difference in Maria's health, and access to healthcare years earlier might have ensured a different outcome. In spite of this, Alicia is not bitter. She never felt entitled, and always accepted that the burden of taking care of her family was hers alone. Although her mother was not told that she was dying, she knew it in her heart and told Alicia that she was grateful for her life. She thanked Alicia for always supporting the family, even from such a young age. Maria died peacefully with a smile on her smooth, unwrinkled face. Those who knew her said that her humbleness and goodness was sincere and pure, like the salt of the earth. She committed her soul to God, gave each of her children a blessing, and passed from the world at peace, knowing that she had the love of her family.

Alicia has no regrets. She thanks God everyday for her many blessings. She accepts her life, the challenges she faced, and she is confident in the knowledge that she did the best she could for her family. Her decisions and actions came from love and a strong sense of family responsibility. During the especially trying times, Alicia would visit the nuns at the church and would look to them for support and encouragement. She knows that her faith in God, along with His blessings and mercies, are what helped her in this life. Her golden rule has always been to do for others. Alicia has a large network of friends, most of whom she has known for years. The niece she raised graduated college with a Master's degree, and has the same strong work ethic as her Aunt Alicia. Alicia does not regret missing the opportunity for marriage and children. She knew that her first duty was to her family, to love and to nurture them. She continues to send money to Mexico for her sister Martha and her family. Alicia enjoys her work as the coordinator of a community food pantry in City Heights. Many seek Alicia out for her advice, guidance and encouragement, respecting her more because of her life experiences. She lives a grateful life, thanking God each morning as she awakens, asking for His protection and guidance, just as she did when she was a young child in that small village in Mexico, sixty years ago.

QUESTIONS

1. What role did Alicia's father play in her life? What was Alicia's mother's role in the family?

2. How was Alicia's character different from that of her sisters?

3. How old was Alicia when she began to look for work? Why did she look for work?

4. Was Alicia's faith in God evident early on in her life?

5. What were Alicia's opportunities for an education and a career?

6. Do you think Alicia and her family were in survival mode? What indications or realizations did Alicia have as she grew up about her family's poverty and struggle to survive?

7. What is a *curandera*? How did the *curandera* help Alicia? Do you believe that Alicia's experience with the *curandera* helped her take a different path in life?

8. Can you relate to moving to an unknown environment in order to find work to support your family?

9. Was Alicia surprised at her aunt's living conditions in Tijuana? Why or why not?

10. Was it easy to cross the United States-Mexico border in the early 1900s? Was the US worried about people crossing over from Mexico? How has this changed?

11. Why do you think Alicia and her cousin risked crossing the US-Mexico border illegally, venturing into a dangerous situation, with no knowledge of the language?

12. If you were in Alicia's place, would you have turned back when you realized how you were expected to cross the border?

13. What do you think Alicia's reaction was when she stayed at the mansion in Point Loma? Was it a welcoming experience for her?

14. Do you think people in a situation of need like Alicia's would easily fall prey to unfair labor practices?

15. Where did Alicia find a place in which she finally felt comfortable and welcome?

16. What was Alicia's experience working in the hotel and in private homes? What challenges did she have in doing this work?

17. What events resulted in Alicia bringing her sister's children and her mother to the US?

18. Did Alicia contribute to the US tax system? Did she turn to US government for any kind of support? Why or why not?

19. Did Alicia have anywhere to go for help and support for her and her family? What were the living conditions like in the neighborhood of City Heights?

20. How do you think Alicia felt once she and her family were granted residency in the United States?

21. Do you think that Maria's health condition would have been different if she had access to preventative care? Do you think Maria would have had better treatment when she was ill if she were an American citizen or had had private insurance?

22. Do you think that health care, like food, is a human right? Why or why not?

23. Why do you think Alicia chose to work in the community and continues to do so even though she has passed retirement age?

24. Where do you think Alicia's strength and determination came from?

Alma's Story

I really have my heart in the work that I do. I have spent years working in underserved communities, and this is where I belong. My goal is to empower people by encouraging them to develop wellness and a feeling of worthiness.

Growing Up
I am a "border girl." I grew up with the best of both worlds: with influences from both Mexico and the United States. I love and respect both cultures. Because of the rich framework of ideas and traditions from both cultures I have the ability to relate to any woman I speak with. I was born in Mexicali into a family of seven children. I am the middle child of six girls and one boy.

My father was a professional boxer, known by the name of "El Pelón Duran." He gave up boxing when he got married, taking a job at the Mexicali traffic control department for a few years, and later moving to a job in a Calexico butcher shop, where he worked for twenty-five years. When I was thirteen years old we went on vacation to Querétaro, a city 120 miles from Mexico City, where my father's family lived. During our visit, my father decided that we should stay and work with his family, who owned a chain of seafood stands. He didn't know anything about the seafood business but that didn't deter him. We all got involved in the business. I remember helping my father push the carts around the streets.

My mother was a homemaker and dedicated herself to this important job. She attended nursing classes to learn how to care for us, and sewing classes so she could make our clothes. I got a lot of inspiration from my mother. She always shared her opinions with us on how we should work to have our own businesses, how we should rely on ourselves and should never be under the control of others. Maybe it is due to her upbringing and personal experiences.

My mother was the eldest of seventeen children. When she was eight years old she went to live with her maternal grandmother in Mexicali. Her grandmother convinced my mother's parents that Mexicali offered an opportunity to attend school, whereas in her hometown there was none. My mother's grandmother was also raising other grandchildren and family members. The respect and priority were always given to the male children. My mother was taught to serve the men of the family and to be obedient in that role. It was very difficult for her, and when she had her own children - all girls except one - she made a point of treating us equally, instilling us with a sense of worth and pride.

I could talk with my mother about everything. She was my dear friend, always very supportive. My mother has since passed away, but I will always carry her nurturing and encouragement with me. My grandmother is still alive, living in Oakland, California with her children. I have family members on both sides of the border and keep in close touch with all of them. My father is still alive. After twenty five years working in the butcher shop, I believe he simply stopped dreaming and became resigned to his life and work. However, since retiring, he has dedicated his life to catching up with his children and grandchildren, and finds joy just by being there for us.

My parents sent all of us to private vocational schools because the tuition at the universities was too expensive. They believed we would have good career opportunities if we had a trade. Both of my parents were very encouraging, making it clear that we must study hard and graduate - there was no other option, according to my parents.

My First Marriage
I completed my degree in Querétaro when I was eighteen. My degree, equivalent to an Associate of Arts degree in the US, is in Business Administration with an emphasis in Hospitality. Querétaro is a tourist town so the opportunities for hospitality work were plentiful. I accepted a job working at the Hacienda Hotel to gain experience in the hospitality field, and enjoyed taking English classes at night and meeting new friends. I lived with two of my sisters and my brother in the house my parents had bought.

My parents decided to return to Mexicali. My dad went back to the butcher shop. My mother would call me every week and encourage me to move to Mexicali. Eventually I did, and I quickly found employment as the purchasing manager for Araiza Hotels, a large chain in Mexicali. I worked until five every day, and then drove across the border to Imperial Valley College, where I was pursuing another degree. Although the distance was only fifteen miles, it would take me a long time to get across the border. I bought a small car and became an expert at weaving through the border lines to get to class on time.

I met my first husband while he was stationed with the military in Imperial Valley. I was twenty-six and had been introduced to him by my friends. We married and moved to San Diego when he was transferred there. My family eventually followed me to San Diego. My husband's family was from Vacaville, California. He was born in Anaheim, just outside of Los Angeles, and military service had taken him all over the world before we met.

The first four years of our marriage were good. We had our first son so I stayed home with him during the day and attended night classes at Southwestern College from five to ten. My husband and I barely saw each other. I continued taking general education classes and finished my AA degree, and prepared myself to return to the workforce. We then had two more boys.

My husband and I had challenges communicating. He did not seek any companionship from me, since he had his buddies to go out with. He was unfaithful on several occasions and when I would confront him about this or other issues, he would only agree with me that we were not getting along. I felt like I had no emotional support from him or encouragement.

My husband was polite and behaved civilized towards my family but he changed when he was upset. Although his family was very nice to me, I found out that he was beaten very badly by his stepfather when he was a child, which marked him for the rest of his life. He was resentful and started to take out his anger on me and our oldest son, by screaming at us when he was upset. Sometimes he would "punish" me for not being "nice" to him by purposefully ignoring me.

I felt trapped but I still stayed in the marriage - I did not want my children to live with divorced parents. My husband became more verbally abusive, then started pushing and shoving me, and he hit me twice. He would constantly be putting me down, saying things like, "Why are you so dumb?" or "You don't know how to be a woman?" He would threaten to leave me with three kids and no job.

I decided to seek help and change my approach. I enrolled in a program that presented statistics about men with behavior traits similar to my husband's. I learned why men act the way they do and why they never change their behavior. I was so surprised, as I had thought all along that I could change my husband, but I finally realized through these classes that it would be impossible to change him. The counselors talked to me and the kids for three months about the situation at home. I also learned what options were available and explored the resources that would help me transition out of the marriage. The program lasted six months. I soon realized that my situation was fortunate compared to the other women in the program.

During the program, I began to talk to my husband without feeling the emotional frustration that I had before. I took control of my life for the first time in eight years. We agreed to a one-year transition period where we would continue to live together but not as a married couple. Meanwhile I would prepare to get a job that would permit me to be home with my children when they got out of school. I no longer expected anything from my husband and we began to transition out of our ten-year marriage.

Taking Charge of My Life

My marriage ended amicably. It was not his intention to destroy me out of revenge or resentment, and I am grateful for that. I realized during that period of my life that I had a choice: I could either hang my head and submit to that way of life, or I could try to overcome my difficulties by improving myself and then my situation.

When my husband left, I stayed in our home with the children. I was determined to improve my life and my children's lives. I obtained certification to enroll uninsured children into the Healthy Families program and worked while my children were at school. In 2001, I started working for La Maestra Community Health Centers, assisting uninsured families with enrollment in the Healthy Families program. In 2003, I received the Local Heroes Award for the work I did in San Diego and for being a role model in the Latino community. The fulfillment from the work I had done and the recognition I received gave me the self-confidence I needed to continue on my path of self-improvement.

I have remarried and am raising my present husband's two daughters. My life now is the way I always pictured it: I have a husband who sees me as an equal, who loves and respects me and our five children. I'm a stay-at-home mom and work independently in my aromatherapy business, in addition to helping my husband with the construction company we started together. Like any family, we have challenges. Right now, construction business is really slow. However, there is one thing that does not exist in my home anymore: violence. We know things will get better later if we keep our hopes high.

I never spoke to my mother about the abusiveness in my marriage because I grew up with domestic violence in my home. I believe that my father saw domestic violence as a normal part of married life and repeated this behavior with my mother. My parents separated in 1998 but they never divorced. When my husband moved out, my father moved in with me to help me with the kids and the mortgage payments. It was great for my boys to have their grandfather help raise them. They spent hours together playing, putting together puzzles and doing homework. My mother lived with my two youngest sisters. We spent our holidays together and our family seemed to be more peaceful after my parents had separated. They actually became friends and would visit each other frequently.

After my mother's death, my father moved in with one of my sisters. He has been diagnosed with Alzheimer's disease and his short-term memory is gone, although his medication seems to help a lot. My father has gotten lost twice so he wears an identification bracelet now. My sister has to make sure that he takes his medication and he walks for one hour each day. Since his time as a professional boxer, my father has never forgotten the power of exercise and he is adamant about following a daily regime. All of my family knows about the challenges of caring for someone with Alzheimer's. It will be continue to get more difficult but we are working together. My two sisters work with me for the same company as well-being consultants. We are fortunate that our schedules permit us to be with our children and take care of our father.

When I think about what I went through in my first marriage, I feel sad and sometimes wish that it would have never happened to me. However, I realize that not everything went bad and I have something very precious from that marriage: my three boys. My ex-husband and I are now good friends and have since asked each other's forgiveness. We are very supportive of each other in raising our children. We have worked out a schedule so he can be with the boys on his days off, taking them to their sports practices and games, exploring nature together and going to all kinds of places.

The children really appreciate him and I admire their relationship. He never had that attention from his own father or stepfather. He was the eldest of five children, the first child from his mom's first marriage. She got married twice and had four boys later with her second husband. I felt so sorry for my husband and wanted to cure the bitterness he carried from his childhood by consoling and nurturing him, showing him how different life can be. The one big mistake I made was to marry him knowing he was abusive towards me before our marriage; I was naïve and thought that he would change. Then I became co-dependent and let my husband take control of my life. I realize this now and I see that this was my own doing and I don't blame him for it. Now I see the changes he has made and I admire him, but I know he would have never done it if I had stayed in the marriage.

I have learned to put myself first. It sounds selfish but when I'm in control, I'm more creative. I believe that we have to do the work of confronting our personal doubts, anger, resentment and unresolved issues in order to clear them away. When I have a positive attitude, many good things come and my days are much more productive. Too often women tell me that they feel depressed and angry with their family situation. They put aside their own feelings and needs to serve their husbands and children, and then feel resentful at how their husbands and children fail to show them respect.

I believe that women have a tremendous responsibility to raise children with the values they need to prepare them for future relationships. My boys not only respect me, they view women as equals. They are not abusive and are caring towards me and their two stepsisters. If I hadn't made the decision to end our marriage, I would have caused a lot of damage to my children.

My parents raised us in the Catholic faith, and I have always had strong faith in God. I have raised my boys in the same faith. I believe in the power of prayer, and constantly ask God for the wisdom to make the right choices in life. There have been some tough times in my life, some more than others, but when I look back I see that none were impossible to overcome. Now when I face challenges, I say to myself, "This too shall pass." I try not to take it so seriously and give it my best effort and faith.

So that's life. I think that we are all born as pessimists to some extent, focusing on what we don't have or what is going wrong in our lives. I have learned through meditation and self-help reading to switch that around. We all have the power to tell our brains how to be a filter and direct what we choose to think and how we choose to feel about life. That becomes our attitude and what we tell ourselves and display to others.

My Work
One morning when my father was living with me and my children, he woke up with horrible back pain. He couldn't move and it was as if all of his muscles had cramped up and his back was bent over. The doctors did not have an explanation for his illness. I called my sister in Mexico and she sent me some natural herbal creams and oils, which we applied three times a day for twenty-one days. The results were incredible. Another time, when I was pregnant I felt such exhaustion and was hardly able to get out of bed. I went to the hospital and they said that there was nothing they could give me since I was pregnant. Again I called my sister and she sent me oils and creams to use. I am convinced that this helped me get through this difficult time. I regained my energy and was able to function normally.

I asked my sister why I couldn't buy these products here in the United States. She explained that the Swiss-based company had not expanded to the USA yet. The company is 77 years old and has been established in Latin America and Europe for years. Nine years ago I heard that the company was finally branching out to the USA and I signed up. It took me five years of training to learn about the wellness products, which I consider to be equivalent to a degree. I worked my way to the position of Director and have 60 wellness consultants reporting to me. I focus on offering presentations and training new leaders. It really is rewarding work for me. I do not consider myself as a promoter of sales products as the products are just a part of the well-being guidance that I offer. I use the products myself and see how they have helped so many people.

For the past ten years, I have been involved in promoting aromatherapy - using natural products to bring calm and peace to stressful lives. This path has brought me in contact with thousands of people, most of them women. I lead "wellness gatherings" in the community three or four times a week, where I talk to women who are interested in taking control and improving their lives. Human beings are more similar than we think - many of the women who attend the talks have the same issues, all stress-related. The gatherings turn into support groups, which are desperately needed in our communities. The fast-paced lives we lead have caused blocks in communication within families.

During the wellness gatherings we offer aromatherapy, foot and body massage and give resources for those who ask for assistance with their problems. As wellbeing counselors we focus on just that, being a guide to those who are seeking wellbeing. We are careful to not provide counseling beyond our expertise. I also encourage women to learn a new career through my seminars in sales, personal appearance, public speaking, and motivational insights.

During the presentations, I try to convey the importance of conquering our internal struggles so that we can be effective in our roles as mothers, workers and members of society. One of the women shared her story about already being a mother when she got married. She was really determined to keep her daughter from being a burden on her new husband, so she worked very hard to bring in extra income throughout her marriage, while raising more children with him. Now the woman's youngest child is already sixteen, and she is angry and resentful, blaming her husband for the missed opportunity to spend time with her children while they were young. She and her husband became accustomed to her bringing in the extra income, but at what price? This woman's situation is similar to many others, and I gave her the advice I give to them. I suggested that she resolve these issues internally and talk openly about what is bothering her to her spouse.

Our lives as women now are different than in previous generations. Women now are expected to work and bring in income to the family, which cuts into their role as housewife and nurturer. Expectations about the roles of family members in our communities need to change. There is a lot of stress caused when the traditional expectations about the role of wife and mother are combined with the role of wage earner.

What I really want ask women is, "Why do you blame your husband? You feared this conflict a long time ago and never spoke about it to him about it. Instead you trained him to think that you are super-human and could do it all. Now you are tired, angry and resentful that you had to endure such a burden." So much of the stress that women feel is caused by not knowing how to communicate, or feeling like it is not the woman's place to be a decision maker. I sometimes find myself reverting into my own cultural upbringing by going to my husband to make the big decisions. Then I stop myself and change the question, so that I ask his opinion but still retain the right to be part of the decision-making process or to make it by myself. This has been a huge transition for me, but one that is right.

A woman once told me that she was absolutely depressed about her family life. Her husband had cheated on her for years but she decided to stay in the relationship for the sake of her children. Her demeanor was downcast and she could hardly look me in the eyes. Her posture, hunched over, betrayed her beaten spirit and lack of self-esteem. The woman was bitter and had carried the burden of that resentment for years. She went on to tell me that, like her husband, her children treated her with no respect. She could not understand how her years of sacrifice had resulted in this situation.

After listening to her, I encouraged her to start by recognizing that she had worth. Until she believed in herself, others would not respect her. I told her to carry her body proudly and to raise her face and look others in the eyes to convey her positive self image. I suggested that she seek counseling to help her deal with her own feelings of bitterness and depression to achieve inner peace. Only with a new attitude and confidence could she begin to change the family dynamics.

She expected me to tell her how to get her husband and children to change. Other women have shared similar stories with me about their husbands' unfaithfulness, asking what to do to keep their families intact. I tell them that if they are willing to forgive their husbands, and truly believe that it will not reoccur, then they need to be ready to really put it in the past and put aside bitterness and resentment. Otherwise, they are doing a disservice not only to themselves, but also to their children, as this resentment will affect their attitudes, permeating into every situation in a negative way.

I always give advice with the sincere intent of helping women to focus on their own internal feelings and desires. Many have never stopped to think about what they want out of life. They just drift into the role of wife and mother and go with the flow. Unfortunately, passive obedience and waiting for things to happen doesn't work. Women need to actively set their goals and establish their own positive self-image as deserving human beings. How can we nurture others if we are tormented within ourselves and have no plan for our lives?

Looking Forward

My own life has really come a long way. Self-development and a yearning to expand my understanding have compelled me to seek the resources that will spark new ways of thinking, bringing more positive energy to my life and to those around me. I listen to motivational tapes while I am driving and devour books about successful people, especially successful women. I have come to understand that, as women, we need to take control of our lives to bring about the changes we desire, instead of waiting for someone to come along and do it for us. Of course there are plenty of external challenges we have no control over. We can, however, control how we choose to deal with those challenges and to adapt our attitude. This understanding has helped me tremendously in my life and is part of the advice I give to others. Reading about women who have conquered overwhelming adversity has empowered me to make changes in my life which were necessary for my well-being and that of my children. I was able to break free from my cultural training regarding what constitutes a good wife and get out of an abusive marriage, and I have never looked back.

I am always searching for balance in my life. I have had to overcome the idea that because of my culturally expected roles as a woman, I don't deserve everything that I want. I need to exercise the right to make my own decisions, obtain the very best experience out of all situations and find happiness and peace in the process of improving myself and the quality of life for myself and others. Each morning I run or walk three miles and clear my brain. I then set my intention for the day. Through this process my self-esteem can flourish and accompany me in my work and my interactions with my family.

My goal is to continue to help the community in the ways that I have found to be effective, focusing on women and their families, offering them positivity and encouragement. I also plan on increasing my team each day and inspiring other women to do the same. Having a business that inspires me to grow each day, not only as a professional, but also as a mom, a leader, a wife, a sister, a daughter and a community member, opens up a new world. I have won trips to different parts of the world such as Switzerland, Prague, Brazil, Argentina, Rio de Janeiro, and other states within the USA. I clearly understand my true role in life and see that there exists a wonderful woman within each of us, but we let our circumstances distract us. We can end up blaming all of our failures on the obstacles we have had in our lives. I am now fully aware that my happiness depends on me and the choices I make everyday have to be directed toward the same goal: to live my life with a purpose: be happy and make others happy.

QUESTIONS

1. What was Alma's family structure as she grew up?

2. What were some of the family conflicts?

3. How did Alma's mother support her?

4. What degree did Alma earn in Mexico?

5. What challenges did Alma face while pursuing a degree in the US?

6. What were some of the differences between Alma's culture and her first husband's?

7. When Alma found herself in a difficult marriage, what did she do to seek help?

8. Do you think that domestic violence is common in marriages?

9. Do you think growing up with domestic violence predisposes women and men to experience this again in their own relationships?

10. What realization did Alma reach regarding her husband's behavior and their marriage?

11. How did Alma support herself and her children as a single mother, after a ten year marriage?

12. What award did Alma receive and why?

13. Why didn't Alma confide in her mother about her marriage problems?

14. What role does Alma's ex-husband play in his sons' lives?

15. What does Alma regret?

16. What values does Alma instill in her children?

17. Does Alma have faith in God?

18. What events convinced Alma to get involved in aromatherapy?

19. How does Alma believe that aromatherapy contributes to overall wellbeing?

20. What work does Alma do?

21. Why did Alma choose this line of work?

22. What are some of the cultural and societal challenges that women who interact with Alma face?

23. How has the role of Latinas as wives and mothers changed in this generation?

24. What tools have strengthened Alma and empowered her?

25. What is Alma's belief about personal development?

26. How does Alma empower other women?

27. How does Alma believe that a women's sense of worth helps her develop?

28. How does setting goals help?

29. What value does Alma impart to those women who attend her support groups?

30. What are some of Alma's goals in working in underserved communities?

31. Do you believe that Alma considers herself to be American?

32. Do you think that Alma has something to offer to society?

33. How do immigrant women like Alma help our country?

Dr. Almansour's Story

Childhood

In 1953, Iraq was under the rule of a young monarch, King Faisal II. In the town of Baghdad, a child was born into a Christian family in a country where ninety percent of the population was Muslim. The child's name was Mumtaz and he lived with his family in the large house his father had built in the primarily agricultural district of al-Mansour. At the time, Mumtaz's house was one of only a few in the area. Since then, the district has experienced significant development. Al-Mansour is a place of embassies and residences for ambassadors and top ranking government officials. The palace of the King's mother, Queen Aliya, is also there.

Mumtaz's father graduated from one of Iraq's first engineering schools in the early 1940's. Upon graduation he was recruited to teach classes in physics and mathematics at the same school he had just finished attending. After leaving the school, he was hired on as a civil engineer with the police department. His job was to build police stations and prisons, including the now infamous Abu Ghraib prison. Mumtaz's father was one of few Christians employed in a top government position.

Before the revolution of 1958, the construction bidding and contracting process was plagued by bribery and corruption. The Iraqi government, aided by Saddam Hussein's uncle, Khairallah Tulfah, awarded whichever proposal came with the best bribes. Following the revolution, information pertaining to the bribes was disclosed to the new government and investigated. Anyone found guilty of corruption in the al-Mahdawi Court was punished and many of the cases resulted in hangings. During one court trial, Mumtaz's father was forced to testify against the government, where Mr. Tulfah still held a high ranking position.

The retribution for bearing witness, combined with his minority religion, made life very difficult for Mumtaz's father and his family. On one occasion, he was nearly killed when a nearby gas station exploded near his building, which caught on fire. While attempting to escape, he was pushed back into the burning building. He managed to evade his attackers, running until he was overcome by smoke inhalation and fear. His heart began to trouble him shortly after that trauma. He traveled three times to the United Kingdom for an angiogram and treatment, but died in 1959.

After her husband's death, Mumtaz's mother, Kawkab, was left alone to care for her four children - one girl and three boys. Kawkab was certified to teach elementary school but did not work outside of the home until her husband's death. Now the sole provider for her family, she began to teach and supported her children with seventeen Iraqi *dinars* per month. Mumtaz was the third of the four children, just six years old when his father died.

Since the Iraqi government provided free education through the university level, all of Kawkab's children attended school. Mumtaz graduated from medical school in 1978; his sister received her teaching certificate and the eldest brother graduated and worked as a mechanical engineer. In 1977, an incident at work changed his brother's life forever.

The brother had instructed one of his employees to adjust a machine, to which the worker responded, "Shut your mouth because you are a Christian or else I will hit you with this hammer." Mumtaz's brother decided it was time to leave the country, and moved his family moved to Detroit, Michigan, where he found employment with General Motors. Mumtaz's other brother also left Iraq, living abroad for a few years, before relocating to the United States in 1978.

History of Iraq in the 20th Century

Iraq is comprised of twenty-one provinces, and three major cities: Mosul in the north, Baghdad in the center, and Basra in the south. Oil was first discovered near Mosul in the early 1900's, and its discovery forever changed the fate of Mesopotamia. Besides oil exports, Iraq is also a large date supplier. Palm dates are grown in Iraq's central region, around Baghdad, and in all areas to the south. The western region of Iraq contains sulfur and phosphates, while the mountains in the north are filled with uranium.

The Turkish Petroleum Company was founded in 1911 with a plan to exploit Mosul oil. In 1913, Winston Churchill, Britain's First Lord of the Admiralty, sent expeditionary teams to the Persian Gulf. The TPC was reorganized in 1914 to include representatives from British and German banks, along with British and Dutch oil companies. From 1914 to 1918 Germany and Turkey attempted to take control of Iraq and the Middle East. They failed; England and France moved in and took control of many of the Middle Eastern countries, including Iraq, ruling them as colonies.

Britain seized Basra, Baghdad and Mosul in an effort to gain control of Iraq's oil.

Three prominent UK figures were influential in the decision to keep Iraq intact: Gertrude Bell, known by the Iraqi people as al-Khatun; Jack Philby, who would later serve as Minister of Internal Security under the British Mandate of Iraq; and T.E. Lawrence, a.k.a. Lawrence of Arabia. These three persuaded Winston Churchill to keep Iraq strong because of its rich agriculture land, its plentitude of oil, and its ideal geographical location. Iraq is also one of only a few countries to border the three continents of Europe, Asia and Africa. The advocates reasoned that Iraq could be a convenient escape route out of India, should the English ever require one.

During World War I, allies Great Britain, France and Russia signed the secret Sykes-Picot Agreement, outlining how they would partition Ottoman Asia after the war was over. The plan included assigning Baghdad and Basra to the British, and Mosul and much of Syria to the French. After the war, with Germany defeated, the partition plans changed. During the 1919 Paris Peace Conference, the League of Nations Covenant entrusted the entire country of Iraq to Britain. This was documented in writing in the 1920 San Remo treaty. Up until 1920, Iraq was referred to as being part of Asia Minor, governed by Sultan Hashmid, and Kuwait was considered to be part of Iraq. Years later, King Feisal II attempted to reclaim Kuwait as part of Iraq but was killed. Each subsequent ruler who tried to reclaim Kuwait suffered the same fate.

The Iraqi people were treated poorly by the British colonial government. By 1920, local outbreaks had begun against British colonial rule. The weapons used were *mejwar*, long sticks with the tips covered in tar. By July, Mosul was in full rebellion and the revolt moved south along the Euphrates River Valley. Iraq remained in a state of anarchy for three months until the Royal Air Force bombing began. Order was restored after reinforcements from India and Iran were enlisted. Bribes were also given to the chiefs of the clans,

Following the six-month rebellion, Emir Faisal, formerly the King of Syria, arrived in Iraq. Faisal was soon proclaimed King of Iraq, and remained on the Iraqi throne until he died of poisoning in 1933. In 1925 the proceeds from the oil revenue from Iraq were distributed to England at 48%, France at 23.75%, United States at 23.75% and Mr. Gulbenkian at 5%.

Faisal I was succeeded by his son, Ghazi. King Ghazi I ruled until 1939. Ghazi assisted the United Kingdom in stopping the Assyrian revolution, promising to obtain assistance for the Assyrians. King Ghazi did not honor his promise to the Assyrians and banished them from Iraq. To this day the Assyrians do not have their own country.

In 1935 Iraq began to refine their oil. Under the IPC (Iraqi Petroleum Company), the British companies, including Mobile and Shell, as well as the French company Elif, were allowed to operate, marketing Iraqi oil to the world. Most of the Christians in the country worked in these oil refineries. The oil revenue brought many riches and developments to Iraq. Infrastructures were instituted throughout the country. The government had more than sufficient funds to support all levels of education, and medical care for all.

King Ghazi's son, Feisal II, was crowned in 1939 at age four after Ghazi was killed in a mysterious car accident. His uncle, Emir Abdul Ila, was appointed mentor to the young king until he reached adulthood in 1963.

Between 1957 and 1958, national democrats, independents, communists and Ba'ath party members joined forces to establish the Anti-Monarchist movement. In July 1958, King Faisal II and his family were massacred during a military coup. One of the architects of the coup to overthrow the monarchy, Abdul-Karim Qassim, assumed the position of Prime Minister of the newly formed republic until he was assassinated in yet another coup in 1963.

Also instrumental in the overthrow of the Faisal monarchy, Abdul-Salam Arif assumed the position of president in 1963, launching a bloody wave of political revenge throughout the country. After turning his back on his Ba'athist allies, Arif was killed in a helicopter crash in 1966. Abdul-Rahman Arif was appointed to succeed his brother following the helicopter accident. He ruled for two years until he was ousted by the Ba'athist coup d'état in July 1968. He was exiled to Istanbul, Turkey.

Ahmad Hassan al-Bakr was appointed as president by the perpetrators of the coup in July 1968. He was believed to be the front man for Saddam Hussein. Al-Bakr officially stepped down from his position as president in July 1979, handing the reigns to his vice president, Saddam Hussein.

Military Service
Mumtaz earned his degree as a medical doctor in 1978. By 1979, he had begun rotations in a variety of medical specialties in different hospitals in Baghdad. One of these rotations took him into the prisons, where he treated prisoners who were doomed for execution. He was assigned to attend a hanging at the Abu Ghraib prison, on a day when many prisoners were scheduled for execution. The *Imam*, or Muslim priest, asked a fourteen-year-old prisoner if he had any last words or requests. The boy

asked to speak with the doctor. The boy pleaded with Dr. Almansour not to remove his eyes after being hung. It was common knowledge that the eye balls of the executed prisoners were removed and sold as organ transplants to the rest of the world.

The boy continued, saying that no one had explained to him why he was going to be executed. The boy came from a very poor family. His father was a drunk who constantly beat the boy's mother. The abuse reached a point where the father supported his alcohol addiction by charging his friends a fee to rape the boy's mother. During one of his father's drunken rages, the boy shoved his father in an attempt to protect his mother from being beaten yet again. His father fell, hitting his head against a rock, and died. The boy did not understand how this accident, occurring in defense of his mother, warranted his execution. Dr. Almansour was so moved by this boy's plight that he advocated on his behalf with the prison guards. He spoke to many but the order remained firm and the boy was executed. His eyeballs were removed and sold by the Iraqi government, along with the others.

Later that year, Dr. Almansour began his mandatory army service of twenty-one months. Two months before his term was to end, war between Iraq and Iran broke out. Because of the war, Dr. Almansour was forced to stay in the military service for an additional four years. Some of this time was spent at the front lines, where he saw many of his colleagues killed or taken hostage.

His first brush with death occurred when he was invited to eat breakfast with his Commander. He dressed and shaved, meeting up with the Commander outside his tent. The Commander noticed that Dr. Almansour still had soap on his face and told him to go wipe it off. Dr. Almansour went back into his tent, wiped his face off and returned to find that his Commander had been killed by enemy fire. His moustache flew off and landed on the flap of Dr. Almansour's tent. If it weren't for the soap on his face, Dr. Almansour would have been killed too. His second brush with death occurred shortly afterward. At a colleague's request, Dr. Almansour had agreed to replace him on dug-out duty. He emerged from the duty to find that his entire unit had been killed.

During his service, Dr. Almansour was ordered to accompany the soldiers to disarm the mine fields. It was widely known that 90-95% of these attempts were unsuccessful, resulting in the bombs and all being blown up. Dr. Almansour protested this order, telling his superior officers that he was a doctor not a soldier. His Commander responded by saying that if he did not do as he was ordered, he would be executed on the spot. With no other recourse, Dr. Almansour set off in the night with ten soldiers.

The procedure involved sending the first soldier into the minefields for the first mile. If he made it through successfully, the rest would follow in his footsteps. Then another soldier would be assigned the second mile, followed again by the rest of the group. This continued until the fifth mile was covered. They would then take photographs of the enemy and return to camp along the same route. Dr. Almansour accompanied the ten soldiers, with no map, with no weapons, among enemy fire. No flashlights could be used, as they would draw enemy fire. Dr. Almansour had no hope of survival and just prayed constantly.

One night, while making the trek, he felt something hard under his foot. The soldiers instructed him to stop in his tracks, keeping the pressure of his foot on the mine so that it would not detonate. One soldier retraced his steps back to the starting point to call for an expert to come from forty miles away and defuse the bomb. The expert finally arrived and rescued Dr. Almansour from his third brush with death.

The fourth incident occurred in 1982 at the Mandali hospital. The Iranians had launched a major attack on the border city where Dr. Almansour worked, capturing all of the survivors. Dr. Almansour could not escape in any direction as the entire city was under siege. There were two water tanks on the roof of every house. He climbed on top of one of the houses and crawled into a water tank. One of his nurses climbed into the other tank. He could hear the soldiers speaking Farsi as they walked by so he knew he had to remain in the tank. He stayed there for more than six hours. Saddam Hussein sent an army force to the city, resulting in heavy bombing all night long. When the shelling finally stopped and he heard people speaking in Arabic, he got out of the water tank and checked on the nurse. She had been killed by the shelling. Although Dr. Almansour had shell fragments in his fingers and toes, he was alive. He was rewarded with three stars.

When the Iran-Iraq War started in 1980, Iraq had vast foreign-exchange reserves in Switzerland. It was two years before Iraqis began experiencing any shortages and the rationing of essentials began. Residents waited in long lines at the local stores. After waiting for hours, Dr. Almansour's family was told the same thing as the other Christian families. "We do not have enough - go to the end of the line." Dr. Almansour traveled from one store to the next, trying desperately to obtain food for his family. Gas was also rationed, and cars were permitted on different roads depending upon whether their license plates ended in odd or even numbers. This increased the difficulty of securing food.

In 1984, Dr. Almansour was released from army service to work in the rural areas. His first assignment was in the Salah ad-Din district, birthplace of

Saddam Hussein. While working as a hospital administrator and medical director, he met Jenan, who would become his wife. They married and settled in Baghdad, where Dr. Almansour worked as an anatomy instructor in the al-Mustansiriyah Medical College. He applied for a scholarship to study in the United Kingdom but was not selected because he did not belong to the Ba'ath political party.

Dr. Almansour left his position at the university to train as an Ear, Nose and Throat Surgeon. He received his diploma in 1988. He worked as an ENT surgeon in the al-Diwaniyah district, south of Baghdad, which was one of the Shi'ite territories. He felt the tensions between the governors and the Shi'ites, with the latter always threatening revenge against the Ba'athist government. Dr. Almansour's fears for his family's safety in Iraq continued to grow, yet he felt the drive to remain in the country and correct the injustices he witnessed under the bloody regime of Saddam Hussein. He protected and assisted many who were being persecuted because of their poverty, their Christian religion, and their resistance to support Saddam.

Saddam Hussein and the Ba'ath Party
Saddam Hussein ruled Iraq from 1979 to 2003. Saddam had been born into a very poor family. He did not know who his father was, and his step-father beat him frequently, sending him out to steal chickens and sheep. Saddam was not successful in school. He seized a handgun from his uncle and took it to school to threaten and, reportedly, kill his teacher. Saddam was ten or eleven when he stopped attending classes.

In 1955 Saddam enrolled in the Ba'ath party. A few years later, he was selected among four other candidates to assassinate Abdul-Karim Qassim, the current ruler of Iraq. Qassim was seen by Ba'athists as being overly sympathetic towards the communist party. After the assassination, Saddam left Iraq and was welcomed in Syria, where he stayed until moving to Egypt to study law.

In 1966 Saddam returned to Iraq. Just two years later, he began preparations for the revolution to overthrow Ahmad Hassan al-Bakr. He assembled a group of loyal supporters, including his own personal army, as well as recruiting body guards from his native district. He became Vice President of Iraq and planned and executed the removal of the IPC, resulting in enormous new revenues for Iraq. Iraq had to look for other markets to sell their oil to as the European countries were angry at being ousted from Iraq, boycotting the Iraqi controlled oil exportation. Iraq found countries like Russia, Japan, and France to begin selling their oil to.

Saddam felt that since he had been the one to maneuver the increase in revenues, he had a personal right to it. Saddam used the money to build his power, demanding that his supporters give their lives for his cause. In 1979 al-Bakr was forced into retirement, shortly after which he was poisoned and killed. It was at this point that Saddam boldly announced to his brother, "Say goodbye to poverty - we will be very rich people."

During the years preceding Mumtaz's decision to leave Iraq, he was exposed to repeated incidents of persecution and torment against colleagues and family members. To guard against retribution, only a handful of them are included here.

The first incident occurred when the Iraqi Minister of Finance received a phone call from one of Saddam Hussein's sons who had suffered serious gambling losses in Monaco. He demanded that the Minister wire him money to cover his losses. The Minister refused, saying that the government treasury was already low. Upon hearing this, Saddam called the Minister to his office, told him to strip off his clothes to his underwear, and demanded that he walk home from his government office. Saddam further warned that if anyone stopped to offer the Minister a ride, he would be executed on the spot. Saddam said to the Minister, "This will teach you how embarrassed my son was, and how you should have sent him the money he requested." The Minister walked all the way home in his underwear, publicly humiliated.

Another occurred when the Chief Dermatologist, who was on-call for Saddam and his family and entourage twenty-four hours a day, seven days a week, was arrested and taken to prison. He was not provided an explanation for his arrest. He was held and tortured for ten days. During this time, the doctor's wife pleaded for an interview with Saddam. After four days, he relented and allowed her visit. She begged Saddam for her husband's life, saying, "My husband has served you well. He is always available to treat you and your family and your officials. What could he possibly have done to offend you?" Saddam responded, saying, "You and your family are allowed to travel at government expense. You have babysitters, and they too are paid for. While in England, your husband sat in a nightclub and talked against me." The doctor's wife asked, "What did my husband say?" Saddam answered, "Your husband was asked what he thought about the war. He responded that Iraq should never have become involved with the war in the first place." The doctor's wife acknowledged the comment, adding "Okay, but you have often expressed the same opinion." To which Saddam replied, "Go get your husband." The doctor's wife went to the prison cell where her husband had been detained to find his dead body. He had been tortured to death. She took her husband's body home to bury.

Still another incident involved Mumtaz's aunt and cousin. They had traveled to the north of Iraq to visit the church ruins there, and were accosted by terrorists. The terrorists ripped the necklaces and earrings off of their necks and ears, and warned them never to return. The terrorists threatened to follow and kill them. They did not sleep for three days after the trauma.

The Ba'ath Party's overzealous enforcement of their traditional dress code was personified when Mumtaz's niece came home one day with her legs painted white. Ba'ath party members had stopped her in the street because her legs were showing. They painted her legs in order to teach her a lesson. Sideburns were also monitored. If men wore them longer than the middle of their ears, members would stop them, shaving a strip of hair from the ear to the top of their head on both sides.

There were multiple incidents involving Saddam's son Oday. He was known to kidnap girls, rape them, and then leave them to be outcasts. Oday and his bodyguards were also known to show up at weddings to kidnap the brides so that Oday could rape them. The would-be brides would then kill themselves out of disgrace. Oday also raised tigers, and he always had three or four of the big cats with him. One day, when one of his ministers failed to follow a command to his liking, Oday invited him to the house. Oday had kept his tigers locked up for a few days, starving them intentionally. When the minister arrived, Oday released the tigers and they attacked. Oday was allowed to do whatever he wanted without any consequences, and he was universally feared.

Two of Saddam's daughters were wed to a set of brothers. The eldest brother flew from Iraq to Jordan to marry Saddam's daughter. At first, King Hussein welcomed him. But when journalists arrived to interview Saddam's new son-in-law about the nuclear arms program he headed, the young man spoke openly about the nuclear weapons Saddam had built up in his arsenal. Following the interview, he realized that he had committed a grave error against his father-in-law, and so began his quest for political asylum. Unfortunately, no country would grant it. The son-in-law was later pardoned by his wife's father, but was the victim of an "accidental" death shortly after his return to Iraq. Saddam of course claimed he had no hand in the death.

Saddam was fascinated by watching people die from his bullets. He would shoot people with his pistol and remain entranced by the blood that spilled out. Saddam custom designed a torture device that would hold a prisoner in a chair between two metal cabinets. To the front and the back of the prisoner were moving doors, each with ten spikes attached. If a prisoner was reluctant to give answers during an interrogation, the spiked doors would rotate closer and closer, a centimeter each five minutes. The spikes would be heated or electrically charged. Eventually, the spikes would bore into the prisoner's flesh in the front and the back. This was said to be Saddam's preferred form of torture, since it was of his own design.

The atrocities in Iraq were not restricted to criminals or traitors, but were even inflicted on those considered to be in the "privileged class". They could never be sure what would happen to them and their families. Saddam's obsessive paranoia affected his reasoning and governed his actions. Saddam eventually had a falling-out with his son Oday, and a lot of people died because of it. Saddam also battled with his sons-in-law. There was no trust between the family members.

United States

During an effort to help hide one of the young girls that was being pursued by Saddam's brother, Dr. Almansour was finally forced to flee Iraq. The fourteen-year-old girl had been told that Dr. Almansour could be trusted to help her escape from becoming another rape victim. He managed to keep her safe by moving her around from family to family. Unfortunately, someone reported his actions to Saddam's family. At that point, Dr. Almansour knew that it was time to get his family out of Iraq.

On July 2, 1989, Dr. Almansour, his wife and their three children arrived in the United States on a visitor's visa. He looked for a job as a physician but says "all doors were closed to me". He was offered a job as a researcher on a project studying Ménière's disease, and was given a J-1 visa for 4 years. During this time he enrolled in a residency program and completed the board requirements to practice family medicine in the United States. His intention was to move to San Diego and set up a private practice where he could serve the community. The process of applying for residency was not automatic, and until his request was granted, Dr. Almansour worried that he would be sent back to Iraq where he would face certain death. Fortunately, he qualified for political asylum in the US.

Dr. Almansour accomplished his goal of establishing a private practice, where he still works part time. He also serves as the Medical Director for La Maestra Community Health Centers. Through this position he is able to develop more services for the underserved communities in San Diego.

Dr. Almansour and his family are not alone in San Diego. There are approximately 30,000 Iraqi refugees and immigrants in the greater San Diego area. They are very resourceful and help one another in acclimating to this new environment. Many have started their own businesses with money borrowed from others within the community. Iraqi immigrants contribute to the US economy and create jobs for others with their businesses.

Life in a new country does not come without its challenges. Adequate health care, language proficiency, job training and placement, assistance with immigration status – these are all realistic concerns facing new arrivals. Additionally, Iraqi immigrants suffer frequent discrimination because of their country of origin. American Iraqis are often victims of hate crimes because they are perceived by some to be enemies, when in fact they have fled from the very atrocities that Americans are fighting against. The immigrants fought to become Americans and take pride in their adopted country. Many of the Iraqis who have settled in San Diego are Chaldean, Christian Iraqis. They are grateful to have the opportunity to practice their Christian faith openly and without being punished as they were in Iraq. The needs of this community are many, which is why Dr. Almansour has dedicated himself to the cause.

Mumtaz attributes his drive and determination to the experiences of his early childhood. He knows that his father's life could have been long and happy, and Mumtaz would have grown up with a father. He was denied that experience, and watched for years as his mother suffered because of Saddam's political regime. He witnessed atrocities and felt compelled to try to help those who had no recourse from unwarranted persecution. Mumtaz's courage enables him to face challenges head-on. His sincerity and adherence to his values have cost him greatly, but his desire to correct injustices keeps him going. While escaping death on so many occasions, Mumtaz could not help but believe that God has protected him and has a greater purpose for him. Not all relocated Iraqi doctors have been successful in starting their careers over here in the United States. The requirements for obtaining a medical license in the US are considerable.

Like their father, Dr. Almansour's children are all pursuing advanced degrees, and have promising careers ahead of them. They see the example set by their father and mother (a licensed pharmacist), not only in their professions, but as responsible citizens and members of the community.

Mumtaz believes that Iraq's future holds promise. He believes that Iraq, being a wealthy country, should adopt policies similar to those in Kuwait regarding ownership rights. In present-day Kuwait, only native-born citizens can open businesses. If a non-native wishes to open there, they must put their business in the name of a Kuwaiti national, granting them a minimum 51% ownership. The non-Kuwaiti native is allowed to hold no more than 49%. This policy insures that control over businesses in the country remains with the Kuwaiti natives. The land and the majority of the revenue also remain in the country. This creates a safeguard against foreign control or invasion.

QUESTIONS

1. Where and when was Dr. Almansour born?

2. What socioeconomic status did his parents have when he was born? How did that change when his father died?

3. What are the largest assets in Iraq?

4. How did the form of government affect the people of Iraq?

5. Why did Dr. Almansour's brother flee from Iraq?

6. When and by whom was oil first discovered in Iraq?

7. What other countries came into Iraq in pursuit of controlling the oil?

8. What decision did Winston Churchill make and why?

9. How was Iraq partitioned during WWI?

10. When did Britain take complete control of Iraq?

11. Who was the first king of Iraq?

12. What was Saddam Hussein's background?

13. What political party did Saddam Hussein belong to?

14. In what year did Saddam Hussein officially take over Iraq? How did he orchestrate this?

15. Why did Saddam Hussein believe that he was entitled to the riches of Iraq?

16. When did Dr. Almansour receive his medical degree?

17. What were some of the experiences Dr. Almansour had during his rotations in the prisons?

18. Which body parts were sold by Saddam Hussein from executed prisoners?

19. Describe some of Dr. Almansour's brushes with death.

20. What was the response of the commander when Dr. Almansour protested against being assigned to the mine fields?

21. When did Iraq begin to experience shortages of food and essentials?

22. After being released from army service, what positions did Dr. Almansour hold?

23. What were some causes of tension in the districts?

24. What were some of the retributions faced by Dr. Almansour's colleagues under Saddam Hussein?

25. How did the Ba'ath party enforce their dress codes for civilians?

26. What was Oday, Saddam Hussein's son, known for?

27. How did journalists find out about the nuclear arms program in Iraq?

28. How was Saddam Hussein's son-in-law's indiscretion dealt with?

29. What fascinated Saddam Hussein? What torture device did he design?

30. How did Saddam Hussein's paranoia affect his relationship with his family and friends?

31. What belief kept Dr. Almansour in Iraq?

32. What was the final incident that convinced Dr. Almansour that he and his family had to escape?

33. How was Dr. Almansour able to come to the US and stay for four years?

34. What did Dr. Almansour do in order to not be forced to return to Iraq?

35. What do you think would have happened to Dr. Almansour and his family if he had to return to Iraq?

36. What are some of the challenges faced by Iraqis in the US?

37. Where in the US did Dr. Almansour settle?

38. What work is he doing to help his community?

39. What keeps Dr. Almansour going?

40. Does Dr. Almansour have faith in God?

41. What are some of the challenges faced by medical doctors from Iraq and other countries when they move to the US?

Dr. Tran's Story

I have a passion for poor people. They really need our help. I especially love the kids. Some of them come into our clinic without shoes and unkempt. I love them immediately and want to help. You should see how happy they are when I talk with them and repair their teeth. I wish I had a video camera to capture their beaming faces as they leave my dental chair. I love the City Heights community, and working here at the clinic. I can't imagine working anywhere else. I could get paid $800 a day working in La Jolla, but this is where I'm needed. This is where I feel at home.

Danang
I was born in Vietnam, in a small city near the center of the country called Danang. I have four older sisters and two older brothers. We grew up in a low-income, inner-city neighborhood, sleeping on the floor of the one room house we rented.

In 1969 my mother received her certification as a registered nurse. She taught classes and worked as a school administrator. When I was three, my mother traveled with a group of cardiologists to Minnesota to be trained in anesthesia. She was away for four long years, leaving the task of raising us children to my dad and grandmother. Once during that time, my mother brought a group of twenty Vietnamese children with severe heart problems to the surgery center in Minnesota for open heart surgery. Of the twenty, eleven survived. When my mother had completed her training, she returned home to Vietnam to complete her residency. She became a professor at the medical school. My mother loved to teach.

My dad worked at the Shell station. Like everyone else in our community, he worked long hours. Most of our neighbors worked in the open markets or on the street, getting up early to prepare food to sell. I learned at an early age just how challenging it was for people to make a living. Too many had little to eat, and I remember how my heart ached for a small neighborhood boy who came around each morning and night, trying to sell hot bread. I begged my mother to buy all that he had just so he could go home and eat. I grew up knowing that I wanted to help people.

Vietnam is rich in oil and minerals. The land in the South is fertile and fish are bountiful. In 1975, the government of South Vietnam was overthrown by the Việt Công from communist North Vietnam with assistance from China, Russia and Cuba. Vietnam provided the pathway for communists to invade Laos and Cambodia.

Việt Công

I was a student at the government subsidized school, and was in the fourth grade when the communists took over. I remember standing on the balcony of my grandmother's home, watching together as the tanks rolled into the city, rifles pointed in every direction. Despite our teacher's best attempts at explaining how our lives would be different now, we were not at all prepared for just how significantly our lives would be changed. The new regime did not provide for meals at school, so we brought our own food, scarce as it was. Seventy percent of the people in Vietnam suffered from malnutrition. My mother did her best to keep our stomachs satisfied with root vegetables like taro and potatoes. Rice was too expensive and meat, too, was a precious treat. We were fortunate if we could have a couple bites twice in a month. Our main daily staple was yucca mixed with grain, and lots of tofu.

I remember when my classmates and I were sent to work on the farms one day a week, tending to the pigs and other livestock. We also worked in the pineapple fields, digging and planting the new plants. For the first time ever we were required to purchase our own books and other school supplies. We used recycled paper, which was very dark and hard to see our writing on, especially by the faint light of the oil lamp I used to study at night. Pencils were very costly, so we made blocks from charcoal and water and used these to write and draw.

We didn't have toys while we were growing up, so we would play with pebbles, stones and empty cans we found in the street. We had no toothpaste, so we cleaned our teeth with salt. We also had no shoes, so we went to school in slippers. A single pair of pants would have to last two years.

When I was in the 6th grade, my sisters and I helped earn money for our family by making fabric flowers from remnants of cloth that we gathered. We would coat the remnants with cooked gluten to make them stiff, and then etch them with flower petal designs. When we placed them over the heat, the petals would curl. We sold the pretty fabric flowers to florist shops.

Our entire city was filled with tension and despair. It was rumored that children who failed to listen or obey in school would disappear, never to be found. If adults were suspected of complaining about the harsh conditions, communist soldiers would come to their homes in the night to take them to jail or kill them.

One of my mother's brothers was in the military service. He worked with the United States armed forces. When the communists took over South Vietnam, my uncle disappeared. Ten years later, one of his friends came to visit our family to tell us that my uncle had been jailed. After ten years, he had attempted escape by eating poisoned yucca to make himself sick. When the soldiers found him so ill, they beat him to death. Years later, this same friend took us to the place where he had buried my uncle.

Another of my uncles was in the United States navy. He was captured and sent to a jail in North Vietnam. When he returned twenty-three years later, he was unrecognizable. He was thin as a shoelace and all of his teeth were missing. Many people were tortured by the Viêt Công, and those who had worked with Americans, like my uncles, suffered the worst. They were chained with big, heavy handcuffs to large stones.

Because my mother had studied in the United States, the communists fired her from her position at the medical school. Her beloved career as a nurse and professor came to a halt. To bring food for our family, my well-educated mother was forced to work in the marketplace, similar to an American swap meet. She would buy cloth and dye it, making curtains to sell. My father also had to find new employment after the Shell station was closed by the government. He found work as a clerk in an electrical store, earning sixteen dong per month – equivalent to less than one US dollar in 1976.

Escape
By 1979 my father decided it was essential that we leave Vietnam. He saw no opportunity for our family's survival under the communist regime, let alone the return to normal life. Although Vietnamese citizens were prohibited from leaving the country, Chinese were permitted to leave by boat. A friend of my father's was Chinese, and was able to help him obtain documents forging a Chinese identity. In 1980 my father escaped to Malaysia.

Upon my father's arrival in Malaysia, he was placed immediately into a refugee camp. The camp was his home until a sponsorship for travel to the United States could be arranged. While living at the refugee camp my father worked as a translator, since he spoke Vietnamese, English and French. He also taught English to the other refugees. Finally, after a three year wait, a church sponsored his travel to Chicago where he began work for the International Rescue Committee.

My father worked for five years, sending money home to our family, until he was able to become a US citizen. Finally, it was time to start the immigration application process to bring our family to the United States. We were unaware that our application had been approved, because the communist government had no intention of allowing our departure. We even had a letter from the United States Embassy stating that we had permission to go to the United States but still, the Vietnamese government refused to let us leave. In the meantime, I successfully graduated from high school, but I knew there was no opportunity to further my studies in Vietnam. In order to survive, we knew we would have to escape.

We planned our escape to include two or three in each group. We traveled to the countryside where we could find space on a boat, paying the owner for each person. My brothers went first, along with some of their friends. The others followed shortly after. My two sisters and I were the last in our family to leave. We found passage on a small boat, along with 92 other escapees. Most of the passengers were women and children. Having successfully escaped the shores of Vietnam, we were now targets for Thai pirates.

On our second day at sea, pirates came up to our boat and threw a bomb made of TNT. It blew up the back of the boat, including the engine. So there we sat, floating, with no way to move ahead, just drifting. Other pirate ships would come by to rob what little they could find. They would typically show up at night. In one day we were robbed ten times. After robbing us, the pirates would seek women and children to rape. My sisters smeared engine oil on my face and in my hair to make me look dirty, grimy and unattractive. My hair stuck out with the dried oil, giving me a crazy appearance.

I will never forget the day the pirates took my friend. She was sitting right next to me when they grabbed her and took her to their cabin. She was raped by seven of them before they threw her back to us. I held her trembling body, while attempting to wipe away all the blood on her. She was in shock and clung to me tightly. All I could do was cry and pray. During the next attack, I held my friend close, terrified of another assault. A large pirate came over and told his friends to take me. My friend and my sisters begged him to spare me, and I was terrified. I remember falling at his feet and begging him to let me be. The pirate pulled me up, put his pistol against my right ear, and pulled the trigger. I thought I was dead. I prayed as hard as I could to the female Buddha, promising that if she saved me that day, I would make something of my life. The pirate left me on the deck as he and his gang climbed back into their boat and sailed away. I lost my hearing in that ear for a long time, and still suffer from nightmares of that day.

One morning, after a month floating at sea, an old Thai man who was working for the Union 76 company came to our rescue, pulling our boat in close to the shore. We'd had no food during the time we were out, and had survived only by measuring out a few drops of water each day along with the sugar and lemon juice drops my mother had made for us in preparation for our escape. Once the old man brought us close, we were transferred to a barge docked just offshore. The Thai government had refused us access and even though helicopters would make periodic drops of sardines, noodles and water, many in our group grew discouraged and anxious about when we would escape. As it turned out, it would be three more months before the government would grant our passage and allow us to depart from the barge. I was just grateful that the pirates would not come in so close to shore, and that the Union 76 workers helped keep us safe. I appreciated the beauty of the ocean and of the crystal clear water, although high tide would leave us water-soaked and coated with salt. The barge was surrounded by sharks, and the pirates still lingered in the distance.

Finally we were granted permission to come ashore and were taken to a camp called Phanat Nikhom, a processing center for Indo-Chinese refugees in the Chonburi Province. Fortunately, our stay there would be relatively short because my father had already obtained our immigration papers to join him in the United States.

Phanat Nikhom
The camp was run by the Royal Thai government and had over 50,000 Vietnamese, Cambodian and Laotian refugees. Each week we received a small ration of food from the camp warehouses. The meat was transported from Bangkok in an unrefrigerated truck, and divided into portions at the camp. Because the camp warehouses also lacked refrigerators or freezers, the food was never fresh and it smelled terrible. The guards had a list of families for each region and would call us by name to come pick up the rations: a small portion of meat wrapped in a bamboo leaf, unrecognizable in appearance and taste, and equivalent to about half of a chicken leg; a fish about four inches long; and some rice. This had to last us all week. In order to preserve the already spoiling food, we would coat it in salt to help it last through the week.

The camp had two markets where refugees who received money from family members already in the United States could shop for more food. They were the lucky ones, as the majority had too little to eat. The more real problem was with water. Each person was allowed a small bucket of water per day. Every morning we would line up with our bucket at five o'clock, and the small ration of water would need to last us for drinking, cooking and washing for the entire day. We would measure off the portion needed for the day's cooking into a clay pot. The rest would be used for drinking and washing. It was impossible to get clean. Even if we could save our entire bucket for washing, there wasn't enough to rinse off the soap. When we left the camp five months later, we heard there were plans to dig four more wells.

There were no bathrooms. The toilets consisted of holes in the ground, about six feet deep, covered by a piece of wood with a hole in the center. There was no toilet paper in the camp so we used leaves, or sometimes pieces of newspaper collected from the discarded food wrappings found near one of the markets. One night a small boy fell into one of the holes, and nearly drowned before we heard his cries and pulled him to safety. He had been buried in the pit of excrement, and we did our best to clean him with banana leaves before the nuns spared a bit of water to wash him off.

The tropical weather was hot and terribly humid. May, June and July were the hottest months, with temperatures ranging between 39 and 42 degrees Celsius. It rained constantly.

There was a separate area in the camp which housed about three hundred Vietnamese and Thai communists, called *irans*. These refugees enjoyed privileges which the rest of the camp did not, like houses with indoor toilets. They dressed as civilians, and enjoyed employment as security guards and received other special treatment. It wasn't clear why they were there.

In our area of the camp, we slept in tents on the floor. My sisters and I shared an area measuring approximately four by six feet. Our tent was connected to other tents, and the roof was made from sheet metal. We had to stay very quiet, as the guards were always circulating. The Thai camp commander, Mr. Cho, was greatly feared. He had one very strict rule, and that was for all refugees to be in their tents by midnight or he would beat them to death. One night my sisters and I were talking and giggling when we heard a loud voice shout, "Who is laughing?" It was Mr. Cho, and the four soldiers who patrolled the camp with him. He ripped open our tent and shined his flashlight on us. Once again I prayed to the female Buddha. Mr. Cho departed our tent without saying a word, and moved on to harass other refugees.

If people in the camp violated the laws they would be punished. The guards were rough, but not usually overtly cruel, as knew they would be reported to the United Nations. Representatives from the UN visited the camp weekly to assist with the immigration process. The UN visitors would listen to complaints, but seemed to lack the power to change very much, and any change took a long time.

My sisters and I were careful to avoid venturing out of the immediate area, especially after nine o'clock at night. The camp guards would accept bribes from people who would come in at night and rob or rape the refugees. We always stayed together at night, taking turns to be on watch for potential attackers. We attached pieces of wood to the bottom of the tent flap to make it more difficult to open.

Our camp had prostitutes who would sell their favors to the Thai soldiers. When they got pregnant, they would have abortions. Although abortions were not permissible in either the Catholic or Buddhist faiths, they were still inexpensive and easy to get. The surgical instruments at the camp were not sterile. Many died from hemorrhage and infection.

There was one small clinic with one doctor and one dentist to serve more than 50,000 refugees. The doctor and dentist were Thai or Vietnamese, and they would rotate, donating their time. There were also Vietnamese physicians who now lived as fellow refugees, and they would help as well. Medications were scarce. There were many children with thin bodies and swollen bellies due to parasites. The children had no sandals or slippers, ate the same rotten food as we did, and had insufficient water to clean or disinfect anything. We ate lots of mint because it was supposed to help kill parasites.

My friend from the boat was also in our camp. After the rape, she was frightened that she might be pregnant. I took her to the clinic and the test came back positive. She was terrified and ashamed, horrified by the thought that the child she was carrying was from the pirates. In the end, we found out that the test was wrong, that she was not pregnant after all.

Inside the camp were a church and a temple, and both were quite beautiful. Every morning, I would wake up at 4:00 am to go to the temple, and after that to church with my friends. Half of the refugees were Buddhist, and the other half were Catholic. The temple held a six foot statue of Buddha made with 24-karat gold, and the incense burned there was said to be of the finest quality. It smelled so good and always had a calming effect. I went to keep myself strong and to keep my hope alive. On very hot days the church and temple would be packed with people trying to stay cool. On those days, I would attend English classes in the morning.

Each day at noon the refugees would assemble in our respective regions of the camp. There were ten families to a region, and for thirty minutes we would meet with the region leader to discuss issues. In this way, the leader was able to manage the peace. Once the noon meeting was adjourned, we would begin to prepare our daily meal.

There were over two hundred orphaned children in the camp, with no one to sponsor or help care for them. Some were newborn babies, abandoned by mothers concerned that their recent change in status – single to double – might adversely affect their pending sponsorship applications. Other single mothers left their children behind in the hope that they would have a better chance at sponsorship if they were unencumbered. Still others were orphaned when their parents died in the camp and there were no other family members to adopt them. I felt heartbroken for them all. Each day after supper was over, I would go to the area where the orphans lived to help feed and bathe them, and to help teach them English. A man named Jim was one of the teachers. He was so appreciative of my work with the children that he gave me a letter of recommendation.

Australia accepted most of the refugees, followed by Canada, the United States and Sweden. The immigration process consisted of a round of interviews at the camp with members of the United Nations. After about a month or so, the applicants would receive notice indicating acceptance or denial. Most denied applications were due to the absence of a sponsor. We were instructed to explain to the interviewers why we wanted to immigrate. Although the most common reason people fled Vietnam was because they were impoverished, it was well known that this answer would not receive a favorable response to their applications. Starvation was an insufficient reason. However, if we answered that we did not believe in the communist principles, we would receive a favorable response to our application, as long as we had a sponsor. Appeals were few, and only successful if the refugee had found a sponsor since the denial. Those who were denied took it hard. Some committed suicide in camp. There was a couple in my region who were denied, so they killed themselves by eating rat poison. Others made the best of the difficult situation, knowing that life at camp was still preferable to life in Vietnam. Those who never found sponsors stayed at the camps until they closed and they were sent back to Vietnam.

United States
Meanwhile my father relocated from Chicago to San Diego, where he worked as a social worker for the County of San Diego, a translator for the immigration department, and a notary public. He secured loans from the International Rescue Committee to pay for one of our three airline tickets. My sisters and I worked in a sewing shop so we could earn enough money

to pay for the other two. When we first arrived in San Diego, we were in a state of disbelief. We had finally made it. It took longer for one of brothers and two of my sisters to join us in the United States. My brother was in a refugee camp in the Philippines called Palawan. His boat had also been attacked by pirates, who robbed and beat him. He stayed at Palawan for an entire year, despite my father's proof that his immigration documents were approved. Two of my sisters ended up in Palau Bidong, a small island off the coast of Terengganu, Malaysia, where they stayed for one year. Palau Bidong was the largest Vietnamese refugee camp during and after the Vietnam War. The refugee camps finally closed in 1991, forcing the remaining refugees to be repatriated to Vietnam. Of course, the Vietnamese government made them suffer for their failed escape. Although Malaysia had secured a promise that the Vietnamese government would not place the returning refugees in jail, the would-be expatriates nevertheless suffered discrimination and ill treatment.

Life in the United States was very different for us. We were very grateful for the chance at a new life filled with opportunities and safety, though in an unfamiliar land. I enrolled immediately in an English as a Second Language class at the adult school in the City Heights neighborhood of San Diego. My English proficiency was poor, and I needed to decide on a field of study. I had always been interested in medicine, and remembered sneaking into my mother's classroom to watch her teach when I was just a small girl. My dream was to become a plastic surgeon but I was afraid to pursue this career because of my poor English. I used to joke with my family, telling them that I would not want to accidentally kill someone during surgery because of my inability to properly communicate.

While studying English, I took a job as a receptionist in the dental office inside a Vietnamese grocery store. There I witnessed how people in pain could find immediate relief. I enrolled in San Diego City College, with the English dictionary as my constant companion for two years. My guidance counselor suggested I take some dental classes at the community college, which would cost far less than at a university. I completed those classes, transferred to San Diego State University, and graduated two years later with a degree in Biology. I applied for a scholarship and was accepted to the pre-dental training program at Creighton University Dental School in Omaha, Nebraska. The course lasted two and a half months. From there, I applied to nine dental schools and was accepted at the University of Southern California in Los Angeles. I graduated four years later, at the age of twenty-six, as a Doctor of Dental Surgery.

My siblings and I all had straight A's in school. Three are now software engineers, one is an electrical engineer, and two of my sisters are biologists. Although we are scattered throughout the country, we all live in the United

States. We have followed my mother's advice – she has always told her children that, no matter who you are, no matter what adversity you face, you must always stay true to your character and keep your virtues strong.

I met my husband, Son, which means mountain in Vietnamese, in French class at San Diego City College. It turned out that we had attended the same high school back in Vietnam. After our second French course he started visiting me at my home. After six visits with my parents, we became engaged. Our engagement lasted nine years while I finished my degree in dentistry, and he completed his computer engineering degree at the University of California, San Diego. We now have a four year old daughter named Katherine, and are expecting a second child. Son and I are lucky to have both of our parents here in San Diego. They help as babysitters and cooks.

Looking Back
I often think back to that time floating at sea, our time on the barge, and to the time in the camp. There were so many perils and discomforts that had brought me to this point. I am so grateful that I have made something of my life. I now know that the United States is truly a land of opportunity, and that if we work hard enough, we will reap its rewards.

When I was seventeen, an uncle took the date and time of my birth and tracked the stars for me. He predicted my future. He predicted that I would be a leader in whatever course I chose, and that I wouldn't be able to run from the responsibility. He told me that I would face great challenges, but would overcome them. Upon applying to dental school my uncle said that I would be accepted, but not accepted. I didn't understand what this meant until the last semester of my Bachelors' degree program. I received a low grade in my last Chemistry class which brought my GPA too low to qualify for dental school. I spoke with my instructor and explained that I hadn't had enough time to study properly for the final exam. He gave me another test, which I passed, allowing me to be accepted into dental school. Everything my uncle told me has come true.

My mother has always prayed to the female Buddha. She still visits the temple regularly. Growing up, we saw evidence of her strong faith and how she practiced her beliefs through her everyday actions. I believe that every religion has good attributes, and all say that you should do good for others.

Looking Forward
I want to continue helping underserved people here in San Diego. It is an honor for me to use the skills I have acquired to make a difference

in their lives. Most of my patients are children and teenagers. I always establish a bond with them by asking about their future and what they are interested in studying. I feel obligated to nurture them and to encourage them to stay in school to achieve their dreams. I never forget that my life was spared, and I intend to keep my promise. Like many others, I have faced enormous challenges. I want to help others who are facing their own challenges.

When my children are older, I hope to join a group of ten other Vietnamese dentists who travel back to North Vietnam every year to provide volunteer dental care. The group stays for three weeks, helping approximately 2,000 children who are too poor to go to school, let alone access any dental care. I have no interest in going to Vietnam solely for a visit, because the communists are still in power. I know people who do go back to visit, but they are careful not to criticize the government publicly. They know all too well that their US citizenship would provide no protection if the soldiers came to take them away. The government states that it allows freedom and independence, but that is not true.

The curriculum in the schools has all changed since my siblings and I attended. Poetry and literature are taught with communist ideals. The Vietnamese communists do not believe in God, so they ridicule anyone who does. The government tells the people mockingly that God does not like the rich while it takes their money away. We read in a Vietnamese newspaper that the monks were being arrested for their religion. The communists worship their previous leader, Ho Chi Minh. His body is preserved in a glass casket, where thousands of people line up to see or to lay on the casket. There are relatively few churches and temples open, and some are being sold to foreign investors.

While I was studying at the university here in California in 1992, I had classmates from Vietnam who were not refugees, but were here on a student visa. They came from wealthy families who were in high positions in Vietnam's communist regime. They paid massive tuitions to send their children to school in the United States. These students drove Mercedes Benz cars, while back in Vietnam, their fellow citizens starved on a steady diet of anti-American propaganda. The double standards were endless for the officials in Vietnam's communist government. After 1975 Saigon City was renamed Ho Chi Minh City. There are casinos, bars, golf courses and more for the wealthy leaders in the party but for the rest, there is starvation. Old people, toothpick thin, beg for food in the streets. Corruption is prevalent and the economy is worse than ever. I can see no hope for Vietnam as long as the communists stay in power.

A note about Dr. Pauline Tran, DDS

Dr. Tran is the Dental Director at La Maestra Community Health Centers. She joined the organization in February 2001 and was integral in establishing the first dental clinic there. The organization currently operates five dental clinics throughout the city of San Diego. Dr. Tran treats all ages, specializing in children's oral health. Through her leadership, La Maestra Community Health Centers, in collaboration with the Anderson Dental Center of Children's Hospital, is home to the first pediatric dental residency program in San Diego. This collaboration created an opportunity for pediatric specialty dental services to be available in the community, including dental care for disabled and traumatized children.

Dr. Tran nurtures her staff as well. She encourages them to seek further training and certifications, coaching them with the same caring spirit she extends to her patients. She is a staunch proponent of preventive care and oral health education. She takes a personal interest in all of her patients, and gets many referrals for children and adults who have experienced previous traumas in a dental chair. Dr. Tran's colleagues are in awe of her success in handling and treating these patients, by turning their fears into a genuinely pleasant experience.

QUESTIONS

1. Where was Dr. Tran born?

2. What was the economic status of her family?

3. What natural resources does Vietnam have?

4. What occurred in 1975 in Vietnam? What other countries supported this?

5. What changes did Dr. Tran experience when the communist government took control?

6. How did Dr. Tran and her siblings help support the family?

7. What were some of the consequences suffered by those who had been supportive of the US?

8. Why was Dr. Tran's mother forced to abandon her career?

9. Why did Dr. Tran's father decide to escape from Vietnam? How did he accomplish this?

10. Where did Dr. Tran's father have to go?

11. How did he manage to send money to his family?

12. How long did it take him to reach the US after he escaped from Vietnam?

13. How did Dr. Tran and her siblings escape from Vietnam? What dangers did they face?

14. How long were Dr. Tran and her siblings on the boat? How did they survive?

15. What traumatic experiences did they face on the boat?

16. Who rescued the boat?

17. How long were the refugees on the barge? What difficulties did they have living on the barge?

18. Who were the refugee populations in the refugee camp?

19. Where was the camp located and who managed it?

20. What was the food like in the camp? How did the lack of fresh water affect daily life?

21. What were the living arrangements in the camp?

22. Who controlled camp life? How was order maintained?

23. What were some of the challenges of surviving in the camp?

24. What health care services were available in the camp?

25. How did people survive in the camp?

26. Can you imagine living under these conditions?

27. What activities were permitted in the camp? What activities did Dr. Tran choose to engage in?

28. Which countries agreed to accept refugees from the camp?

29. What happened to those refugees whose applications were denied?

30. How did Dr. Tran and her siblings arrive to the United States?

31. What course of study did Dr. Tran choose to pursue in the United States? Why?

32. Was this easy for her?

33. Can you imagine having to survive through the trauma that Dr. Tran faced before arriving in the United States?

34. Can you imagine having to pursue a career in dentistry in another country, in a foreign language?

35. What were some of the values Dr. Tran learned from her mother that have helped her accomplish her goals?

36. How does Dr. Tran hope to help the children in Vietnam?

37. What changes have happened in Vietnam in terms of education and how the United States is viewed?

38. What were some of the double standards for the elite of the communist party in Vietnam?

39. According to Dr. Tran, what needs to happen in Vietnam for the living conditions to improve?

40. Why did Dr. Tran choose to serve as a dentist in a non-profit organization serving low-income families?

Elena's Story

I have arrived at a point in my life where I am doing things that are really important to me. I work with women. Not just any women, but truly destitute women – women who have been forced to leave their countries behind for the sake of their children. One of the things I saw while growing up was that women were the best managers. Women could make do with almost nothing. My mother was a great example of this. Even when it seemed like there was nothing to eat, she would figure something out. My mother raised chickens and she would barter, trading the chickens for supplies for our family. I remember thinking then that if a woman could do so much with nothing, how much better could she do if she had even a little bit of money? Everything my mother did was for her children –nothing was for her. When I wanted things for myself, she would call me selfish. Thinking back, I know my mother was right. I also know that that I am where I am today because of my mother's upbringing. She helped me to understand why the women I work with are here in this country, why they put their own needs and desires aside. It is all for their children.

It was July 1969 when I first came to the United States. I was in the states on a visitor's visa from Belize. A friend of mine, a fellow teacher from Belize, convinced me that I could study at Tulane University. She believed I was smart enough, perhaps too smart to remain in Belize. She was concerned that my ideas would not be popular in Belize. She promised to help me to get settled in New Orleans, offering to let me stay in her home, help me find a job and learn my way around. When I arrived at the airport in New Orleans, my friend was not there to meet me as we had arranged, and I knew immediately that she would fail to keep the rest of her promises.

I was a stranger in a strange land with only 125 dollars cash. I found a phone book and worked my way through until I found a boarding house with a vacancy. The weekly rate was 35 dollars and included two daily meals. It was a large boarding house, with women on one side of the house and men on the other. On my first night at dinner, an attractive young man politely asked if he could take the seat next to me. The young man's name was Evristo and he told me about how his parents had brought him from Cuba when he was only two months old so that he could grow up in the United States. Evristo was very sociable, and at breakfast the next morning, he announced to everyone that I was the woman he would marry. Of course I was caught completely by surprise. I had just arrived and had yet to determine my next course of action since my well made plans had fallen apart so abruptly.

On my first Sunday at church, the priest introduced me to the Perrin family. Mr. and Mrs. Perrin offered me a job as a live-in with them and their seven children during the week. On the weekends I would return to the boarding house where Evristo would always be waiting for me. He showed me around New Orleans and we became well-acquainted. In December I decided to go to Boston where some people I knew lived. I requested a week off work to make the trip. While seeing me off at the airport, Evristo asked why I would want to leave New Orleans. I explained that I had come to America to better myself and to further my education. While in Belize, I had earned top grades in school, in English, Theology, Spanish and Bookkeeping. I had even taught classes in Spanish and Bookkeeping while there. So, while I was extremely grateful to have a job with the Perrin family, it did nothing to help me achieve my goals. Evristo replied by saying, "Look, you don't have to worry. Marry me and you can stay in my apartment and continue your studies. You won't have to worry about your immigration status or your visa expiring." I agreed, and Evristo and I married the next October. I moved into his small apartment and we lived together as friends. By that December, I learned that Evristo had been married previously, and had a child that he had failed to mention. So I returned to Belize, and Evristo followed me there. Evristo met my family and we talked everything over.

On the advice of my father, I returned with Evristo to New Orleans and for the first time, we began living as husband and wife. The year was 1971. While I was away Evristo had sublet one of the rooms to an older gentleman, a former professor from Michigan. And while I didn't much care for the fact that we had to share our home with a stranger, the man taught me a lot about life in America. Evristo was a calm and sociable man. He enjoyed parties and spending time with his friends, most of whom were Cuban and Honduran. We had very different opinions about life, the most important of which were our goals for the future. I wanted more out of my life, while Evristo was content with his job as a welder and his life filled with parties and friends. Evristo was a true-blue friend. He would come to a friend's aid at any hour on any day if asked.

I gave birth to a son, Aldo. Two months later, I decided it was time for me to go to work, in spite of Evristo's being adamant that I should stay home with our son. The professor who still lived with us was named Charlie. He taught me how to compose a resume and how to apply for a job, as well as how I should present myself. He explained to me how to differentiate between dead-end jobs and those that had opportunity for advancement. He also recommended that I avoid spending too much time with Evristo's friends so that they could not take advantage of me the way they already did with Evristo. When I was ready to start my job search, I found a woman nearby to care for Aldo. I would wait for Evristo to leave for work early in the morning, then I would get myself dressed and take Aldo to the caregiver's. I applied for a job as a health educator with the Louisiana Family Health Foundation. I was offered the job, and while attending the orientation, I was surprised to meet someone I knew, Betty, who was the sister of Mrs. Perrin. She was apparently also a foundation trustee. She greeted me by name and talked with me. From that point forward, the clinic director was leery of me because of my acquaintance with a foundation trustee.

At the beginning, I managed to keep Evristo from finding out about my job. But at the beginning of the second month, things started unraveling. The Honduran neighbor who had been watching Aldo refused to answer her door. She was not comfortable being a party to deception. After that, I took Aldo along with me, leaving him under my desk as I worked. Next, Evristo's car broke down, and he returned home that morning on the bus. I called my supervisor to explain why I could not come to work. She refused to excuse my absence, so I had to tell Evristo about my job. At first he was furious that I had deceived him. But after a few hours he calmed down, asking what I had done with my earnings. I told him that I had put all of it in savings. Now Evristo was able to repair his car, and reluctantly accepted that I would continue working.

I really enjoyed my job as a health educator, even though it included educating teens and their parents about birth control. This was hard to reconcile with my religious beliefs. This did, however, bring me back to my feeling that I was selfish. Back home, I had watched as two of my aunts, with sixteen children each, would come over constantly to borrow flour, sugar and other food while our family rationed what little we had. I felt then that it was more of a sin to bring more children into the world than could be provided for, than to prevent them through birth control. My friends back home felt my ideas were not suitable for Belize. I had already given up Catholicism because I disagreed with some of its practices. Here, in my job as a health educator, I observed things in the community that made me think differently about life. Ninety percent of our patients were African-American, and there were so many pregnancies, most of them teenage pregnancies. Many of the teens were angry, angry at life in general. I wondered if their parents had spent more time with their children, if the kids would be less angry at life.

I decided to change religions, and began attending a non-denominational church. I liked what I heard, what Pastor Marvin Willis had to say. The majority of the congregation was African-American. Pastor Marvin's message was about education, and about where the people lived, and how they were living. He told them that if they would educate themselves, they would become free. He told them that a life on Welfare was the opposite of freedom; it was actually a subtle form of bondage. Pastor Marvin told his congregation that a life in the projects was not a suitable way to live, and that it was merely a way to keep the population segregated.

The housing projects where many of the congregation lived resembled tiny cities, with clinics on the first floors, and stores across the way which all accepted food stamps. They sold different merchandise than what could be bought downtown. There was absolutely no reason for tenants to venture outside of the projects. Generations of families grew up there, separated from the city and the greater New Orleans community itself. Pastor Marvin began setting up businesses in his low-income community, like landscaping, construction and roofing. For the first time a woman could become a roofer if she wanted. He then turned the companies over to the workers, showing them that they could become private business owners with all the benefits, responsibilities and control associated with ownership. At that time, Welfare was set up so that a single parent would receive more than a married couple. Pastor Marvin explained to his congregation that if both the husband and wife were working, they wouldn't need Welfare at all. He empowered women and the whole family benefitted. In the early 1970's, home computers were not common. Pastor Marvin purchased some for the church, encouraging the children to learn to operate them.

In the meantime, Evristo became increasingly unhappy with my work, my religion and my ideas about life. I did not fit in with his partying friends, just as Charlie, our tenant, had warned me. I began to realize that we really had nothing in common. There were so many things that we could not discuss without getting into an argument. Evristo finally returned to school to take his GED exam. Unfortunately, it didn't have any effect on his ambition. He refused to better himself further by enrolling in career training programs of even looking for a better paying job.

Not long thereafter, my position as a health educator was changed to that of a case manager. My boss, Doris, continued to feel threatened by my acquaintance with Betty and the Perrin family. She believed that I was a threat to her position. I didn't enjoy the deskwork as much as I had working with people in the community, so I resigned from my position with the foundation. I responded to an advertisement for an English as a Second Language teaching position for illiterate adults. I had to perform a demonstration, and I was offered the job. In addition to teaching, I conducted Best Practices workshops and seminars for other ESL teachers. The job required quite a bit of travel. I hired a live-in housekeeper to take care of Aldo and our home. I was then promoted to job developer. I loved the work. I had the ability to uncover job openings in places where most other job developers never thought to look. I had a knack for noticing companies, even those advertised on trucks, and would call to inquire about potential openings for my clients. It was very rewarding.

Meanwhile, Evristo's unhappiness increased. When I found out I was pregnant with my daughter, Evristo declared that he was not the father. He made me feel the same way I had when my great-grandmother told me that my ideas about life made me less of a woman. He said, "You are either not female enough, or you are too much woman and are messing around with other men. Otherwise you would not think and behave as you do." He started to behave very peculiarly. Each day, when I arrived home from work, I would need to look for Evristo. The housekeeper would say that she saw him come in, but that she did not know where he was. One day, when I opened my closet to hang my clothes, Evristo was waiting inside. When I asked what he was doing inside the closet, he said that he was waiting to see the man I brought home. Another night I was tired to go searching for Evristo in the closets, so I went straight to bed. When I woke the next morning, I found him under the bed – again, waiting to see another man.

The pregnancy was very difficult for me. The doctor warned me that my baby could be born mentally retarded, so I had that worry to add to my concerns over Evristo's increasingly odd behavior. Evristo was changing jobs frequently. I had become friends with the managers and colleagues at work who were also job developers. I would ask them for leads for Evristo. They helped him out with referral after referral. It was embarrassing that Evristo would not keep the jobs that had come as favors from my coworkers. Finally, my patience was at an end. I said, "Look Evristo, the next time you lose your job, we will separate." Evristo had threatened constantly that he would kill himself if I ever left him. It always worked. I stayed as long as I did because he told me how guilty I would feel for causing him to take his life. He continued by saying that the guilt of having caused his suicide would keep me from succeeding at anything. The emotional abuse always worked, and I would always give in.

After the birth of our baby girl, Evristo lost yet another job. I couldn't take anymore. I told him, "That's it Evristo! I am leaving you this time for sure." Evristo replied as he always did, "Elena, this is my last day on this earth and it's because of you." I had heard it so many times, that something in me snapped. I told him that the choice was his, and that if he was determined to kill himself, then I could not stop him. I told him that I refused to be held hostage by his threats one day more. I told him, "My life does not belong to me. It belongs to the children and I have to do what's best for them."

Over the years, I had pleaded with Evristo to get professional counseling, to talk with someone who could help, but he didn't listen. After awhile, I finally gave up. There are things I will regret for the rest of my life, but on that day, I could see no alternative other than to leave. I knew that if I gave in again, the lives of my children and myself would be forever manipulated by threats and blackmail. Evristo went to get his gun, which mercifully did not work. Next he went to the drug store and purchased a variety of over-the-counter medications. He swallowed several in front of me. When he had done this before, I always called the ambulance, the police, friends, neighbors, whoever I could think of. This time I did nothing but repeat to him that the choice was his alone. Evristo asked me to come and lie down next to him while he died. I told him "No, if you are intent on killing yourself, do it alone." I took my children and I went to the zoo. I refused to allow my son to witness yet another drama by his father. I knew that if I stayed, I would once again give in to Evristo's threats. We were gone only an hour. When we returned to the house, Evristo was dead. I looked down at him and instead of feeling sorrow, I was filled with incredible anger. I said aloud to him, "You son of a bitch, after all that you have put me through, now I am responsible for burying you!"

It would have been much better if we could have divorced. Evristo's life would have been saved and our children would have had a father to grow up with. I called the police, told them what had happened and showed them the empty bottles. Of course they asked me why I hadn't stopped him, and I did my best to explain his history, how he had kept me hostage with his threats for years. The police launched an investigation; Evristo's family in Florida threatened to sue me for not stopping him; and all of his friends blamed me for his death. It was horrible. A social worker came to talk to me about the trauma that Evristo's suicide had caused me. She let me know that I did not have to go back to work and recommended that I apply for Welfare. I asked her "Who gave birth to these children? As far as I know, I did, not the government. They are my responsibility." I probably wasn't thinking very clearly at the time, or I'm sure I wouldn't have been so rude to the social worker. Obviously she was only trying to help. The community where I lived seemed to turn against me. After all, Evristo had been a warm, calm and always friendly man, who was very generous with his friends. They told me that Evristo was dead because I was too proud, too materialistic; always wanting more than I had, and trying to be something I was not. I responded by saying that if they wanted to talk about me, they could help me first by paying my bills and my rent. And if not, they didn't have the right to talk.

I acted horribly toward everyone. I told them not to expect to see me mourn or to dress in black. At Evristo's funeral, I asked the mourners, "Why do you speak of Evristo as though he was such a good person? You are talking about a coward, someone who took the easy way out - a very selfish person." What Evristo did to our family was worse than when he abandoned his first child in Tampa, Florida. He moved on, and acted as though the child never existed. With our children, he made the choice to take their father away entirely. I couldn't forgive him. I no longer thought of Evristo as a person. I was consumed with how to face daily life, raising two children on my own.

God has always been with me. Just two months earlier, before Evristo's strange behavior began, he brought one of his friends to our house. The friend was selling insurance and burial plots. We each took out life insurance policies, so that our house would be paid for in the event that either of us died. At that time our house cost $12,000. When Evristo died, I used the money to replace my broken car. Of course this only served to add fuel to Evristo's friends' hatred. Looking back, I know I could have done things differently. Since that time, I have learned about suicide and alternative ways to deal with people who are suicidal. Besides encouraging Evristo to seek counseling, I didn't know of any other ways to deal with his threats.

I came from an extremely poor family, and a culture that did not believe in divorce. My main concern was daily survival. There was no time to talk, or to think about anything else. People in my country believed that education was something that came from a book. No one ever spoke of suicide when I was growing up, and I never heard of anyone killing themselves. I had absolutely no frame of reference. When I left home, I was like a horse with blinders on. I had one thought only - that more education would get me out of the life I left back home.

As a child, it was difficult getting up each morning to see how my mother and father struggled to put food on the table. My mother would get up early every morning to cook and bake so that it would be ready in time for us to go out and sell it, bringing home just enough money for breakfast. Her pots were smoke-stained black because she cooked over an open fire. The fire would be lit each morning, and stoked throughout the day so that she could keep cooking and keep baking. I knew there had to be an easier way of life. My father would purchase sacks of pumpkin seeds for my mother to toast. Then my siblings and I would go out at night, with cans on our heads, to sell them. We would measure out a penny's worth of seeds using an empty match box. When we had sold all of our seeds, we would come home. My parents always sent the same three of us, because we had the best sales skills of all the children. We would strategically place ourselves at the ticket counter just outside the theater. I would tell the ticket buyers, "You will want to snack on these seeds while you are enjoying the movie." There were other sales people as well, and we would sometimes get in fights over territory. My sisters and brothers who did not excel in sales as well as the three of us were sent out to deliver orders of cakes and other food. My mom would make bean fritters with sauce and we would take them to school to sell during morning recess so that we could bring the money home at lunchtime. Then we would take something else to sell during the afternoon recess. My parents were very strict about homework, so we had to hurry and finish that before we were allowed to go out at night to sell.

There came a time when my father did not have the six dollars to pay to the government for the "hire-purchase agreement". The hire-purchase agreement was a program for landowners to obtain materials from the government to build a house. So my dad, who was very practical, rented a piece of land for five dollars, built a small house and we all moved there. He knew that he wouldn't have enough money to buy a new set of clothes for our birthdays, Christmas and Easter, so my father divided up the land between all of the children. He taught us how to plant seeds, water and tend to our crops and then told us that we could keep the money made from the sale of the corn, beans and vegetables. We were very motivated to produce good yields from our crops, and were able to earn enough to buy ourselves the clothes that we needed. He taught us a good lesson, and found a new way to produce income for our family. My dad always worked. He had a job at the Public Works Department earning fourteen dollars per week sweeping and maintaining the streets. When the sugar cane industry came into our district, one of my uncles was hired on as a supervisor, and he brought my Dad on at thirty-five dollars a week. My uncle was considered very savvy, because he had finished the 8th grade and continued to read a lot. Besides his regular job, my father would also plant and harvest other people's fields.

My Dad was from Belize. We knew very few of his family members. They were of Mayan Indian and European blood. His grandmother spoke only Mayan, so we had to learn the language in order to communicate with her. My great-grandfather had come to Belize as a school teacher from some European country. My father had his white skin and green eyes. My cousins on my father's side are all fair skinned with green or honey colored eyes. We spent far more time with my mother's side of the family. They had a very close bond, and were proud, in a positive way. No matter how black they were, they would always introduce each other to their friends and neighbors. They were proud to be black. My father spoke very little about his family, but my mother spoke often of hers. Every year, she made a point of taking us around to visit all of our family members on her side, of which there were many. She wanted to be sure that we knew all of our relatives and kept up our communications with them. When I went back to visit not long ago, I continued the tradition by taking my granddaughter with me. It seemed like we were always on the road with my mother, visiting all of our relations.

My great-grandfather on my mother's side was directly from Africa – more specifically from Nigeria. He was brought to the West Indies along with lots of other slaves. Those that were considered rebellious were shipped to Belize. My great-grandfather earned his living in Belize as an "Obeah Man", or voodoo priest. At that time, missionaries were arriving in Belize from Ireland and Scotland. One of these Scottish missionaries was a school teacher named Emily Durand. It was said that she hated black people. Every morning as she passed by on her way to school, my great-grandfather would greet her. And every morning – at least, at first – she would just ignore him. After awhile she responded to him, saying, "Don't talk to me, you are black." My great-grandfather said to his mother, "I am going to fix her".

Next my great-grandfather invited Emily to dinner, but of course she did not come. So my great-great-grandmother took the dinner to the school and asked another teacher to give it to Emily. On the very next day, my great-grandfather waited for her to walk by and said, "I will wait for you. Within one week you will come to my house on your own." And sure enough, she did as he said and they ended up married. Of course my great-grandfather had no doubt that waht convinced her to change her mind was the spell he put on the food that she ate. The two had many children, and all had dark skin and blue eyes. My grandmother married a six foot tall Portuguese man named Ismael Noble, blending our family bloodline even more. I have cousins who live in New York that people believe are French because of their skin and eye color. The boys are all fair skinned with blue eyes, and all of the girls are dark. In Belize we are considered to be mulatto, a person of mixed white and black ancestry. In New Orleans, if you have one part in thirty-two that are African, you are considered black so I have always considered myself African-American.

I have one relative that doesn't look like any of the rest of us. She is very black. When I took my granddaughter to Belize for a visit, I was worried about how my granddaughter would connect with her. She asked my granddaughter, "Do you know who I am?" And my granddaughter responded, "Yes, you are Mar." Children take people at face value, and do not feel the need to categorize others until they are older and learn it from someone else. If we had told my granddaughter that Mar is black, then she would have thought of Mar in those terms rather than as the person that she is. Mar is Mar, regardless of her color. My granddaughter confirmed this.

When I was a child, my Aunt Isabel came over to visit with her three-week-old baby boy. She asked my mother if she could leave him with us for a few hours. She didn't come back for twelve years. My Aunt Isabel's lived life like a gypsy. She moved around a lot. My parents raised the boy, Otto, as their own child. My mom told him that his mother was Isabel, and when Otto would ask who is father was, my mom would always say, "When you grow up, I will tell you." When Otto turned eighteen, he came to my parents and told them that he needed to go to his mother. "It is not because I do not love you, but I need to ask her some questions", he said. When he found Isabel he asked, "Why did you give me away?" "Because I could not afford to keep you", Isabel replied. Otto became very angry and argued with his mother, accusing of her of lying and saying, "You had other children before me, and after me, and you kept those." Otto came home and recounted his unhappy meeting with Isabel. My mother did her best to console him and help him to reconcile the answers that Isabel had given him. My mother said to him, "Otto, when you were born, it is true, your mother could not afford to care for you. By the time she was ready to reclaim you, we had already become attached and she knew we would never be able to give you up." Otto felt satisfied with the explanation, knowing for a fact that my parents loved him and had nurtured him all of his life.

Otto was very fortunate to have been raised by my parents. His siblings did not fare so well. Five of the twelve are in jail, three for drug-related crimes, one for armed robbery and one for grand theft auto. The other seven are professionals. One disappears on a regular basis. Otto was still insistent on knowing who his father was. My mother kept searching for the information and finally, six years ago, she was able to take Otto to meet his father. By then Otto was a grown man with seven kids of his own. My mother had tracked down the father of Isabel's first and third children from their birth certificates. Strangely, that line was left blank on Otto's, her second child. My mother naturally assumed that the man had fathered Isabel's first and third children had also fathered Otto. She went to him saying, "Pedro, I want to bring your son to meet you." He argued with her for awhile, but she was insistent and he finally gave up. She took Otto to meet Pedro, and Pedro said, "I never knew that you were my son. I don't know if you are, but if you want me to be your dad, then OK."

Otto was not the only child left at my parent's house. They had seven natural children and six more that were "drop offs". Two of the six were not even related to us. So we were thirteen kids altogether. My parents treated all of us the same. They raised us all as Catholics and paid the tuition to get us all through school. My mother and my father both rose for the six o'clock mass each morning.

After Evristo's burial, I took my children and returned to my parents' home in Belize. It took two months until I was ready to go back and face my life in the US. My parents insisted on keeping Gina with them in Belize for awhile, because my dad said I needed some time to get my life back together. I had a live-in housekeeper to help take care of her at my home in the states, but my parents said that she would be better off with them. I could not refuse. What my dad said was law. My parents had always told us kids that when we left home, we would have to send one of our own kids to take our place. Gina was born with a skin disease that caused her skin to peel off. She also had asthma. She did not cry for the whole first year. I left her in my parents care and returned with Aldo to New Orleans.

Upon my return to work, I was met with a startling welcome. It was my first day back to work, and during lunch, my boss's wife, Rosa, practically accosted me in the parking lot. She accused me of having an affair with her husband and of breaking up her marriage. I was shocked and upset, and returned to my office to confront my boss. I asked him what his wife was talking about. It turned out that on the day he learned of Evristo's death, he told his wife that he wanted to separate from her because he was in love with me. We did have a good working relationship and he was a great help to me. He had always been friendly, but I never suspected that his feelings were anything other than that of a boss for his subordinate and the situation caught me completely unawares. He went on to tell me that now that I was free, we could finally be together. Aside from my obvious surprise, I was in no condition to get involved in a serious relationship, and I certainly did not want to be the cause of a broken marriage. I told him that it was not to be, and over the next few days we decided that it would be best if he left the agency. Of the two, I definitely needed the job more than he did. He never did return to Rosa, his wife. Rosa was from a very wealthy Honduran family – one that owned a lot of stores where we placed workers. This created another challenge. My boss was replaced, and all of my supervisors were from the Honduran community. They went out of their way to make my life at work uncomfortable since they thought I should have quit instead of my boss. So I started looking for another job.

A few years later, when Gina was three years old, I was out one night at a club with some friends, and that's where I met Mike. As we entered the club, the six-foot, four-inch bouncer stepped forward, telling the owner that he would pay my entrance. Not long after we stepped inside, Mike reappeared in street clothes. He had apparently taken the rest of the night off. He asked me to dance, but I refused. Being American, I didn't think he would know how to dance salsa, but I soon found out that I was wrong. As it turned out, Mike was a salsa instructor. We started dating and married soon after. His parents and sister were wonderful; they very welcoming of me and my two children. Mike's mother was from a coal mining family in West Virginia, and his father was a college graduate. Mike's aunt was a dean at U.C. Berkeley. Mike's parents' backgrounds were very different, and although they had been married for years, they had stayed together for the sake of their children. Mike's mother told me that her husband had had an affair with another woman, and since that time they decided to live together but not as husband and wife. I think this had a significant effect on Mike and his sister Cathy. Cathy never had any boyfriends and she never married. Mike had never been married before me. I believe that his attraction to me was in part due to how different I was from his parents. I think Mike's parents had given up on having any grandchildren. When I became pregnant with Yvette, they were thrilled.

When I first met Mike, he was a bum. He went from one soccer field to the next, and since his sister Cathy always gave him money, he really didn't have to work very hard. Mike and I shared many interests. He loved books and I called him a "walking encyclopedia", just like his father. We talked about books, visited museums and attended the symphony. He had graduated high school with honors, but did not go on to continue his education. After we got married, I encouraged him to return to school full time. His family was also very supportive.

During my marriage to Mike, I met some very interesting characters. One of them, a psychologist named Dr. Francois, helped open the doors to some very interesting jobs for me. Through one of his clients, who just happened to me the Mayor of New Orleans, I landed a job as an English language instructor in the Haitian English Language Project. One of the conditions of my employment was to learn the Creole language. Dr. Francois taught me for four months.

During that time, Haitians were coming to New Orleans in droves. As I learned more and more about the Haitian culture, I felt compelled to become an activist. I organized protests in front of the jail and raised funds to help pay the legal fees. Dr. Francois helped get the Haitians released from jail through his relationships with the Parish government. I translated for the Haitian detainees and the Haitian community members, while helping with job placement. At the conclusion of the project, I was offered a job at the Royal Sonesta Hotel. I had made many contacts placing Haitian workers there. The hotel hired me to work in the Human Resources office, and while there, the executive housekeeper, Ms. Jessie, befriended me. I asked to be transferred from Human Resources to housekeeping and through Ms. Jessie's guidance, I quickly learned many new skills.

The people at the hotel were great to work with. They were dedicated and so very friendly. Ms. Clark was English, and Ms. Jessie was African American, and both had worked for the hotel for more than twenty years. Despite the fact that neither had proceeded past grade 7 in school, they were self taught and extremely efficient. One day Ms. Jessie said to me, "Elena, I'm going to teach you to make a bed in three moves."

The housekeeping department actually made money for the hotel. The hotel's general manager was appreciative of the fact that I was willing to put on a uniform and clean rooms when needed. I used this to my advantage, like the time I brought my idea about instituting a monthly Employee Recognition Breakfast. He was supportive, and allowed me to ask our vendors to donate gifts for the event. Our department continued to increase profits and customer satisfaction for the next six years that I worked there. Then Mike took a job with the State Department, operating as a liaison between the Customs and Border Patrol departments. He was assigned to work in Pharr, Texas, a little border town where the most significant event during the five years that we lived there was when the new Wal-Mart opened. I applied for work at the Wal-Mart, was hired and started training, and on the third day there, I quit. I took issue with the minimum wage pay, and the daily humiliation. Each morning, prior to the store's opening, the employees were gathered into a circle to chant Wal-Mart's praises. New employees were forced to make up new pro-Wal-Mart tributes. At first, I thought the ritual was just for new trainees, but I quickly learned that it was required of all employees.

After I quit Wal-Mart, I stayed home with my kids for two months. I applied at a jewelry store in the next town over. I didn't know anything about jewelry, but quickly learned how to assess stones and the settings. There was considerable competition between the four sales people there, and I soon learned that working on commission paid a lot better than working for salary. My childhood sales training came in handy and I sold $8000 in the first week. They made me the Diamond Sales Manager. One day a man came into the store and said he needed to buy some gifts. I found out that he was carrying $50,000 in cash, so I didn't let him go until he had purchased some diamonds and a Rolex watch. I found out later that he had been laundering money, but at the time, I was just told to sell.

We kept in close contact with Mike's family and agreed to meet in a central location each weekend so they could take the kids. My cousin's husband wanted to come to the United States, so I convinced Mike to let him stay with us until he got a job. Mike wasn't too keen on the idea, but reluctantly agreed. On the third day after he came to live with us, my daughter Gina came to tell me that the man had taken her from her bed to his the night before. Gina, who was thirteen at the time, threatened to scream so he let her go. I confronted him and he left the house. I was afraid to tell Mike, so I just packed up the kids and went back to New Orleans. Mike believed I had left because of my experience at Wal-Mart and my small town boredom. Back in New Orleans, I went to work for a school district and formed a parental involvement group. The general theme was that education was the path out of poverty. At first, the parents in the migrant families were reluctant to participate because they felt they were too poor to contribute anything. I showed them ways that they could contribute, like painting the school and showing other children in the school how to grow and tend to crops.

One of the first people I looked up after I returned to New Orleans was Dr. Francois. He was pleased that I had returned and told me about an opportunity to teach English as a Second Language, help develop the curriculum, and conduct job training for a grant program. He let me know that the program was riddled with problems, and that I was just the one to take on the challenge.

Mike left Texas and came back to join us in New Orleans. His next assignment was to the Bahamas, so we went through the security clearance process, packed up and moved overseas. The first week there I started getting sick. I had pains in my stomach which the doctor insisted was amoebic dysentery because I was not accustomed to the food and water. I was sure he was wrong since we bought all of our food and water at the commissary. The second doctor told me the same thing. The third doctor was only five minutes into the exam when he ordered me to go to Miami for a colonoscopy. I went for the colonoscopy and woke up a week later. They told me that I had colon cancer and that it had spread to my other organs, like my kidneys and lung. They surgically removed parts of my colon and other organs. I returned to the Bahamas on the 17th of February 1991. It was customary for the telephone to work only a couple of hours each day, and they were not working that day at all. I felt an urgency to speak with my mother in Belize, and when I finally reached her she asked me, "Who told you?" When I asked what she was talking about, she explained that my father had died at 4:00. At 12:00 that day, my Dad had asked my mother to call all of us kids to come home. He had asked, "Where is Pasha?" That was the nickname he called me. "Why can't she be here?" he insisted. My mom did not want to tell him that I was sick. My brother had spent over a year in the hospital with colon cancer, and my father had sold his business to pay for my brother's treatment. Shortly after my brother was released from the hospital, my father got really sick. By the time he sought medical care, it was too late. Colon cancer took my father's life.

My mom didn't know how she would get the money to bury my father. She wasn't really involved in my father's business and knew only that he had invested in stores along the Mexican border, and that they were financially comfortable for the first time in their lives. She would watch my father dress up and polish his shoes twice a week to go to the bank. She would make fun of him, saying "Somebody's an actor." She would ask him what role he was playing and in which movie. My dad would just laugh. One of my cousins tried to get my mother to open a bank account once, but my mother simply replied, "Why bother? Whatever your father has is mine too." So when my father died, my mother had absolutely no idea what money they did or did not have. My mother went to our cousin Ariel, who owned a funeral parlor. He told her not to worry, that my dad had come in just a few months before and had picked out a particular coffin and that he, Ariel, would take care of it. My mother did not want everyone to be sad, so she decided to forgo the overnight vigil. People came from all over, bringing her food and company. A couple came by and said, "Vida, you probably don't know what a generous man your husband Aurelio was. He lent us $10,000 when we needed it, and now we are returning it to you." Then there was a woman who came and gave my mother $5000, saying that my father had brought her baby milk from his stores for years when they didn't have enough money for milk and food. By the end of the evening, my mother had received more than $40,000.

All of my sisters and brothers were there. My foster brothers and sisters grieved differently because they realized how much my father had done for them even though they weren't his blood relations. They offered to take care of all the funeral expenses, but my mom told them that it had already been taken care of. So they just gave her money. Thanks to Mike's connections in the State Department, we arrived six hours later. The funeral looked like it was for a dignitary, and the procession was over a mile long. My son was enlisted in the Navy and was stationed in Korea at the time. With the help of the US Navy and the Red Cross, Mike was able to locate Aldo so that he could fly in for the funeral.

After the funeral I went to Miami to begin a month of chemotherapy. Mike took the kids back to the Bahamas. The night before the start of my chemo I had a visit from my dad. I woke with a start at 3 am to see my father standing by my bed. I asked him, "Papi, why didn't you wait to die until I could go to see you?" "Don't worry Pasha," he replied. "I am not angry with you. Your sister Tita told me that you were sick." He started to walk away, but I stopped him, saying, "Wait Papi. Let me come with you." He answered, "No, Pasha, it is not yet your time." And then he disappeared.

I started the first round of chemotherapy the next day. At the end of the month of daily treatments, I returned to the Bahamas where I continued to receive radiation and chemotherapy three times a week for a year. It was the hardest year of my life. I lost my hair, my finger and toenails, and my teeth would fall out when I tried to brush them. My skin turned very dark and I hurt all over. I vomited constantly. All I could do was laugh at my situation, and I would tell people that I was running on spare parts since my organs, or at least portions of them, had been removed during surgery.

I believe it is critical to teach our children about God. Once taught, that seed will always be there. My parents taught us all to know and love God. During the year of my treatments, that faith kept me from ever doubting my recovery. Sometimes when the nurse would come to visit, I would overhear her telling the housekeeper that she didn't know if she would be back the following week or not. She didn't have faith that I would live. As if it weren't bad enough to lose my hair, my fingernails and my teeth, in the ninth month I went blind. I couldn't see anything. It was a side effect of the chemotherapy drugs. The physician said that my cancer evaluations looked good, so he was sure the treatments were working.

Mike was absolutely wonderful during the year of hell. He would take the kids to work with him, turning it into an adventure when he inspected the planes and documents. He would often bring me along in the car so that I wouldn't be left by myself. No matter how our marriage ended, I would always be grateful to Mike for the care he gave me during the whole ordeal. On February 26th, a full year into my treatment, I decided that I had had enough. I was through with chemotherapy, radiation and medication. As I lay down to sleep that night, I remembered how the prophet had come to Hezekiah in the Old Testament. The prophet advised Hezekiah to get his house in order because he was going to die on the following day. Hezekiah thanked the prophet for the message and did what he could to get ready for death. Then he recalled the legacy from King Solomon. Hezekiah kneeled down and with his eyes facing east, he prayed, "God, listen to who is talking to you. It is Hezekiah. I have lived according to your words, please help me." So I did the same. I said to God, "God, listen to who is speaking to you, it is Elena."

I reminded God of all the good things that I had done in my life to help others. I reminded him of the special commendation I had received from the Pope for taking a woman and her baby in from the street. Mike and I had been driving by and noticed two women with a baby just sitting on the curb. They seemed to be in pretty bad shape. We stopped and asked if there was a problem. They explained that they had come from Honduras with $20,000 cash in hopes of curing their baby. Mike and I drove them to the hospital where they had just been rejected. After ten hours of advocating and waiting, the staff finally admitted the baby into the hospital. The baby, who was falling in and out of a coma, was diagnosed with encephalitis. The mother and her sister stayed in our home for three months until the baby was well enough to travel back to Honduras. Sometime later, the women visited the Pope in Rome, and that's how I came to receive the special commendation. So I proceeded to remind God of this and of the other good works I had done. I asked Him to be merciful to me. I asked God to either heal me, or take me before the break of the new day.

When I woke up the next morning my eyesight was restored. I called to my children, and told them that I could see. My daughter Yvette said, "Mom, you are delusional! What color dress am I wearing?" I laughed aloud, describing her attire to the last detail. We were all overjoyed. I had been in bed for the past three months, and on that day I got up and started living again.

Soon after, Mike was transferred back to New Orleans and subsequently discharged from diplomatic service. We were without income, and I blamed myself for Mike's dismissal. I was sure that my illness had caused Mike to miss too much work. I called our friend Bill to ask if he had an apartment where we could stay temporarily. Bill was so generous. He invited us to stay in the apartment above his, in a very nice area of New Orleans. It was the only residential building in an area surrounded by businesses, which made it very peaceful at night. On the first day, I called on my old friend Dr. Francois. I was a fright to see, as my hair and nails had not yet grown back. In spite of my appearance, Dr. Francois said to me, "If you are ready to work, we are ready to hire you." I started immediately, working for the refugee program at the YMCA. The staff there was extremely supportive. By 2:00 in the afternoon, I would grow very tired. The others would take turns teaching my class so I could rest for a bit. I continued to work and support our family for the next 18 months.

In the meantime, Mike went on trial and was sentenced to time in jail. He was released in 1997, reinstated, and assigned to a new post in San Diego. His job was to track down illegal aliens and make them talk. He would methodically analyze the intelligence reports, pouring over them late into the night. Mike was very good at his job. He enjoyed interrogating people who were suspected of visa fraud. He did not give up until he found their employers, and prosecuted them. He told me that he enjoyed watching people squirm under his interrogations. I often wondered how we could get along coming from such different backgrounds and working in such different worlds. I always gravitated towards jobs that helped refugees and immigrants to gain a better life in this country. Mike's job was to prevent them from entering, and track them down if they did. His sister would joke with us saying, "Mike tries to keep them out, and Elena tries to keep them in."

We had only been to San Diego once before. We hadn't really liked it. It didn't seem like the people were very friendly, at least not when compared to New Orleans or Texas. We had hoped that Mike's new assignment would be in New Mexico or Washington State. Now that we were in San Diego, we agreed that I would take some time off work and go back to school. Of course, this was not meant to be.

One morning as Mike was looking through the classified section of the newspaper he said, "Look at this ad. They are looking for you." It was a position for an ESL and VESL instructor. I hadn't even unpacked. I called and scheduled an interview for 10:00 the next morning. I waited for over two hours, observing the chaos around me, with phones ringing off the hook. Finally a woman came out and asked who I was. I explained that I was waiting for an interview and asked if she would like me to help answer the phones. I answered phones for the next three days. On the third day I was called into the CEO's office. He asked what I was doing there. I explained how I came to be answering the phones, and he offered me a position as a job developer. There were four other job developers, and they were all men. At the end of the first week I heard one tell another that I wouldn't last long because I was doing "man's work". At the end of the first month the CEO asked each of us for a report listing our caseloads and refugee placements. I began calling the businesses where my fellow job developers had supposedly placed refugees. It was disheartening. Many of the so-called placements were to businesses that were closed, some for more than a year. I went to the CEO with the information, suggesting that he make a few calls of his own. I did not want to be the sole bearer of bad news. He verified my findings and became very angry. There were no supporting documents for placements from any of the other job developers. In the month since I had started, I had placed thirty refugees into jobs – all were Cuban. The CEO fired one of the developers the same day.

During the second month of my employ at the resettlement agency, the county conducted an audit. They took my case files and quickly realized that the sampling was of Cuban refugees only. They asked for samples from the other job developers, but of course there were none. The county gave our agency one month to straighten out the mess. The CEO gave one of my charts to each of the three remaining job developers to use as a template. Two of them quit outright since it was an overwhelming task to chart evidence of their last year of work. I suggested that the CEO ask the county for one additional month so that I could try to straighten it out. I worked 22 hours a day for the next two months. I tracked down refugees who had come through our agency during the previous year, and built case files detailing their employment. I visited the companies during the day, and at night, I made calls to the refugee workers.

Mike was not happy with my inattention to our marriage. Mike was a neat freak and wanted me to be with him 24 hours a day. He accused me of wanting my job more than I wanted him. He started drinking, which really surprised me. Mike and I were both very busy with our work, and we grew apart emotionally. As his drinking got worse, he became abusive. I threatened to tell his supervisors about his physical and emotional abuse, and Mike admitted himself into rehab.

At the end of the two months, the county returned for the follow-up audit. The auditors were pleasantly surprised to find everything in order, and I was immediately promoted to Assistant Director. I surveyed the entirety of the organization while evaluating the needs of the community. I began applying for grants and the agency started to grow.

During the time I worked at the resettlement agency, I traveled to Africa to research the possibility of opening an office in Kenya and Uganda. During one of my trips, I stopped in Dubai for a week between connections. I was surprised to see how the women were dressed, covered entirely in black, with iron masks to cover their faces. My second surprising observation was the kind of television programs that the women watched. They were Spanish daytime dramas, dubbed into Arabic. I soon realized that their fascination stemmed from the hope they gained from the stories. The common theme surrounded servants who would end up in marriages to wealthy men. When I attempted to board the plane to come home, I was detained and taken to jail. For two days I was unable to find out the reason for my detainment. Finally they allowed me to purchase a phone card, and I called home. Mike contacted the American Embassy, and although it was closed for the day, he was able to reach an American who came to see me at the jail, and translate for me. I was released into the custody of a female guard who sat with me at the airport until my plane departed. She explained that I was detained for walking around without proper coverings for my body and face. She warned me not to make the same mistake again.

I worked at the agency from 1997 until 2005, but during the last three years of my employment, the CEO and I had different opinions on the direction for the agency. Some of our best grant writers became disillusioned and left because of their dissatisfaction. The agency started to experience financial difficulties, so the CEO made the decision to cut everyone except me, the CFO and himself to part-time. I told him that I was uncomfortable with his decision, and chose to transfer to a different location. I contacted him to let him know that a large grant opportunity was available, and asked if I could work with the grand writer to develop the application. He agreed, promising me that I would receive a raise in salary if the agency was awarded the grant. Despite fierce competition, our application won. The CEO broke his promise and I threatened to leave. Personnel at the county learned of the turmoil, and advised the CEO that my involvement had been a major factor in the grant being awarded to our organization. I resigned from the agency, and the program was eventually defunded. I was sorely disappointed that the efforts of so many talented individuals had been wasted.

Two years after I separated from Mike, I met Fausto. He was a good influence on me at that point in my life. He helped me to learn how to relax and appreciate life. Living with Fausto taught me what it would be like to live in the US illegally. We were constantly vigilant for fear of Fausto being detained and deported. I soon realized just how much we take for granted. I experienced first-hand the daily survival issues faced by people in Fausto's community. Fausto remained calm. He would visit me during my break at work just to bring me coffee. He never pressured me about anything, never judged or criticized me. We got along very well. I was especially appreciative of this after the abuse I had suffered from Mike during our last few years together.

My children's reaction to Fausto was not positive. They did not feel that Fausto was "nice" like Mike, and asked why I would be with him. Fortunately, they had not been around during the last years with Mike, so they were not witnesses to his abuse. Yvette had seen it just once, and told me that I should not tolerate it. Gina and Fausto fought continually, even though they did not speak the same language. Gina spoke only English, and Fausto only Spanish. My son Aldo never visited while I was married to Fausto. All of my children are still devoted to Mike. They visit each other frequently. I too maintain an amicable relationship with Mike.

In 2005 I began working at La Maestra Community Health Centers. I became involved in a variety of projects and programs, all focused on assisting immigrants and refugees. One of my favorite projects is managing the microcredit loans. I believe that my success is due in part to my time with Fausto. I lived in a community where people, like my mother, could make a living out of nothing. I watched as people learned to survive in a hostile environment - an environment unfriendly to illegal aliens. When I was assigned the microcredit project, I knew immediately which neighborhoods to target first. I was proficient in the languages and I knew just what it would take to make the program work. I had learned it decades earlier, selling roasted pumpkin seeds and baked goods from my mother's hearth in Belize.

My children are all grown, and moved out of the house years ago. Yvette is twenty-eight years old. She is very tall with red hair and black eyes. She is extremely independent, and speaks her mind like her grandfather and aunt. Yvette is enormously talented. She paints beautifully, she sings, and she loves to be around people. She attends the university and works in New Orleans. Aldo also lives in New Orleans, where he works full time. He is also in the National Guard. Aldo is very outgoing. He married a Columbian girl and they have three daughters. Aldo's in-laws were not supportive of the marriage because of Aldo's black blood. Aldo is light skin, but they did not want their grandchildren to have black blood. When Aldo and his wife divorced, his in-laws did not want their granddaughters to associate with our side of the family. So we get to see the girls through pictures only. Aldo has since remarried, and has another daughter with his current wife.

Gina went to Belize at age eighteen to live with my mother. When she was twenty-four, Gina became rebellious, informing my mother that she was going to move in with a girlfriend. My mother drove Gina to the airport, and when Gina asked who was traveling, my mother responded, "You are". That is how Gina ended up living with me in San Diego.

Life presently seems to consist of a series of tragedies. Sometimes I lie awake at night, thinking about the events of the past two years. But a voice deep inside reminds me of the principle that has guided my life for as long as I can remember - the gifts that God granted me are not for my own good, but for the good of my fellow man. Along with these words comes the consolation that I am still in obedience, and that good things are in store for me.

I am reminded of the women that I work with, of how their lives have been a struggle not for just two years, but forever. I think of Lidia, a refugee from Cuba, came to this country in a boat. She risked her life to get here, and the fact that she is legally blind did not deter her. She says that death and life in Cuba are the same thing. To her, being in Cuba was a form of death. If she died at sea, at least her suffering would be over. Lidia and I met in 1998 when I was teaching English as a Second Language. She wanted to start a business of her own, but she had no money and no idea how to conduct business in America. La Maestra Family Health Centers partnered with a local foundation to initiate a microcredit program. La Maestra's program is modeled after Grameen Bank, founded and managed by Dr. Muhammad Yunus.

Lidia presented her idea, and on the surface it seemed impossible because of her blindness. She proposed going to Los Angeles to buy surplus merchandise and reselling it at the swap meet. I asked how she would get to Los Angeles, and she replied, *"Hermana, si vine de Cuba y estoy viva como no voy a ir a Los Angeles que es aquí mismo"*. (Sister, if I made it all the way from Cuba and I'm alive, how would I not be able to get to Los Angeles which is just nearby?) Her loan for $250 was approved.

Lidia travels to Los Angeles by train, buys her merchandise and then transports it to the swap meet on the trolley or bus. The bus drivers all know her, and help her to get on the bus with her bags of merchandise and table. She does not limit her sales to the swap meet, but instead moves from person to person on the trolley. She tells them that she is on her way to the swap meet, but can sell them anything they'd like right then and there.

The microcredit program has a savings component built in. When Lidia paid off her loan, she was given proprietorship over her savings. She opened a bank account, and you would have thought that it had a million dollars. Lidia is now a US citizen with a bank account. She boasts about having achieved the American Dream. Lidia is on her third loan, and has hired two women to work for her. She supplies them with merchandise, and tells them how much money she expects back. If they sell it at a profit, then the profit is for them to keep.

I think of Minerva, who immigrated only recently after waiting many years for her visa. She came with her seven year old son. Her sisters encouraged her, promising to help her until she found a job and could afford an apartment of her own. A month after she arrived she was told that she could no longer stay with her sister and her family. Without a place to stay, she and her son moved into her car. Minerva became very depressed. She would park at the beach so her son could at least enjoy some recreation. Minerva's son would encourage her, telling her to pretend they were on a picnic. It was at the beach that a member of one of the microcredit groups met her.

Laura told her about La Maestra and how it could help her. Minerva came and introduced herself, but did not immediately share the details of her situation. It was only after the second session that she opened up and told us that she was living in her car. She did not want to return to her country because she had sold her business, and all of her belongings. She explained that she had been a professional masseuse and relaxation therapist for over fifteen years. One of the women offered her a room, and another recommended her to a friend. That referral turned into thirteen massage appointments just that week.

Minerva did not have money to buy the equipment she needed to do massage therapy. Through La Maestra's microcredit program, Minerva is now in the process of establishing a massage and wellness practice here in San Diego. In addition to the loan for $250, we raised another $240 as a group, and gave it to her.

Another woman that comes to my mind is an African refugee named Adama. I first met Adama when she arrived here with her seven children from Liberia. She was the second wife and did not belong to the same tribe. When her husband found a third wife, he wanted to take her children and give them to the new wife. Adama ran away with her children and hid. She applied for refugee status and was brought to the United States.

She did not want welfare, she wanted a job, but Adama was illiterate. I challenged her to learn to write her name, address and telephone number. I promised her that once she learned that, I would get her a job. She came to my office everyday to practice. One day she said, "Look Ms. Elena, I can write my name, address and phone number. Where is my job?" I kept my promise and found her a job.

When Adama came back, she talked to me about how she had earned her living in Africa. So I introduced her to the microcredit program. Adama wanted a loan so that she could do what she had done in Africa. When she paid off her first loan and received her savings, Adama bought a dining room table. I had known Adama for two years and was unaware that she and her family were without a dining room table. I asked her why she had not told me that she didn't have a table, and she responded by saying that it was more important to have food and a roof than a dining room table.

Adama continues to struggle with housing because of the size of her family. Watching her make ends meet with a job that paid $10 an hour was nothing short of amazing. One of the most important things for Adama is to have a little money saved in case they should have to leave in a hurry. This concern is born out of her experience in Africa.

Another group I work with through La Maestra is low-income seniors. I help place them in volunteer jobs that benefit the community. Through a collaborative program they can qualify for up to twenty hours of pay each week. This helps them not only financially, but gives them a sense of purpose as valuable members of society. The community benefits from their experience and maturity.

My hopes for the future are that I can learn to think, speak and act in accordance with the principles of harmony and peace within me. I hope that as I bind myself to the goal of helping to better the lives of the people I serve, I can do so with kindness and purpose. I hope there to be no discord, no envy or unpleasantness, and that creative intelligence will lead and guide me in everything I do.

QUESTIONS

1. What country is Elena from? How did she come to the US? When? Why?

2. What situation did she face upon arrival to the US?

3. Was Elena educated in her native country?

4. Under what circumstances did Elena meet Evristo? Why did she decide to marry him?

5. What were some of the differences between Elena and Evristo?

6. How did Elena fit in with Evristo's friends?

7. Who guided Elena in finding work after her first child was born?

8. Was Evristo supportive of Elena working?

9. What challenges did Elena face in working?

10. What misgivings did Elena have in her work as a health educator? How did Elena deal with that inner conflict?

11. What examples from her family did Elena recall to help her accept her job duties?

12. Who were most of Elena's clients as a health educator?

13. What made Elena change religions?

14. What were some of Pastor Marvin's messages that resonated with Elena?

15. What effect did public housing in New Orleans have on the poor?

16. What programs did Pastor Marvin create to empower his congregation?

17. How did Elena's husband react to the changes in Elena's philosophy, beliefs and career?

18. What other work did Elena take on?

19. Was Evristo's behavior rational when Elena was pregnant with their second child? What were some of the challenges Elena faced with her husband's behavior?

20. What was the threat that Elena's husband used repeatedly to keep Elena from leaving him? Do you think that Elena believed his threat to be a bluff?

21. Why do you think Elena stopped preventing her husband from attempting suicide?

22. Why do you think Elena was so angry at her husband when she found him dead?

23. Did Elena apply for government assistance to raise her two children after her husband died?

24. How was Elena ostracized by their friends and community?

25. Did Elena have a frame of reference from her home country or family regarding suicide?

26. What two things did Elena believe would see her through difficulties and pull her ahead in life?

27. What family structure did Elena grow up in? What was her family's economic situation?

28. What skills did Elena and her siblings learn early on in life?

29. What cultures was Elena's father from? How was Elena's mother's family different?

30. What values did Elena learn from her parents?

31. Where was Elena's maternal great-grandfather from? How did he arrive to Belize?

32. How did Elena's great-grandfather intermarry into another race?

33. What race does Elena identify herself as? Why?

34. How does Elena's family deal with the various races in the family?

35. How many children did Elena's parents raise?

36. What was their religion?

37. Why do you think Elena returned to Belize after her husband's suicide?

38. Was her family supportive?

39. What situation did Elena encounter when she returned to work in New Orleans? How did this affect Elena's work?

40. How did Elena meet her second husband?

41. What did Elena and Mike have in common? Did this relationship differ from her first marriage?

42. What challenge did Elena have to overcome as an English language instructor with the Haitian English Language Project?

43. What advocacy did Elena do on behalf of the Haitians in New Orleans?

44. What job did Elena take after the ESL project ended? What skills did she learn there?

45. Why did Elena move to Pharr, Texas?

46. Why did Elena quit her job at Wal-Mart?

47. What incident caused Elena to move back to New Orleans? What work did Elena find?

48. Why did Elena move to the Bahamas?

49. What illness ran in Elena's family?

50. How did the community in Belize show their support for Elena's family when her father died?

51. How did Elena come to peace over her father's death and not being able to be present?

52. How long did Elena undergo chemotherapy? What were the side effects?

53. How was her husband supportive of Elena during her illness?

54. How did Elena end up moving back to New Orleans?

55. How did Elena end up living in San Diego? What work did she find in San Diego?

56. What did Elena find out about her coworkers and employer?

57. Why did Mike and Elena drift apart?

58. What were some of the cultural differences that Elena experienced in Dubai?

59. 59. What new concepts did Elena gain in her relationship with Fausto?

60. 60. What career did Elena eventually settle into? What does she value the most about this work?

61. What are some of the commonalities between the women in the microcredit program?

62. What is Elena's hope for the future?

Fabienne's Story

I am realizing now that I have blocked out many aspects of my childhood life. But I still can call up a few memories of my neighborhood and surroundings.

Bangui

I remember growing up in an emerging and quickly growing neighborhood of Bangui, the capital of the Central African Republic. We did not have a school or a church in our neighborhood. So we walked about two miles to the next town up to go to school. On the way to and from school, we would share our food and learn to play together.

The school year runs from October 1 to June 30. There are only two seasons in the country: a dry season from October to March, and a rainy season from April to September. Every year, there is a brief period of rain in mid-February that lasts about a week or two and is said to bring fish to the rivers and ripen fruits, especially the mangos. The road to school was lined with mango trees. These belonged to nobody in particular. So from the middle of February to the end of school in June, we gorged on mangos at their different stages of ripening. In February or March we would carry salt and small knives in our bags because the fruits were green, hard and sour. By May, we would carry water in whatever container we could find, because the mangos had become soft, juicy and really messy. The boys would climb the trees and drop the mangos down for us girls to catch. Then we would share.

When the season of mangos was over, it was the season of sugarcane and pineapples. We would rummage through the sugarcane plantations and cut what we could eat. Although the fields were privately owned, all we needed to do was send one spokesperson to ask permission of the owner. They never refused. They would just direct us as to which tree or which area of the field they didn't mind us pillaging that day. In return, we never took more than we needed, and we tried to leave the place as clean as we could.

I remember always having many girlfriends. My mother would rather I serve as a host to my friends than go visit them in their home. So I was almost always inviting a few friends over. I learned from my mother to always cook for more people than expected: "Always cook big dishes, because you never know who might show up unexpectedly." My closest friend was Marianne, until her death at the circumcision camp. Marianne lived next door, so she could stay with me until late. She usually ran back to her house only when our eyes started to close by themselves and my mother shook us awake. Marianne's mother and father were both drinking heavily, so on most days there was no food in their house, and nobody cared whether she came home on time or not. Marianne had two older sisters but they lived with family members far away in two different towns.

Like all girls around the world, we had our maternal instincts and inclinations that guided us when we played. However, we did not have dolls to play with. I remember that until the age of 9 or 10, I did not have a doll. After that, I would regularly receive dolls in school as a reward for good behavior or for good grades. There is a kind of grass that grew in the backyards and around city dwellings and it has hairy roots. We would uproot the grass in our backyard, wash off the soil and braid the hairy roots. We would then cut fabrics and make dresses that we put on the "body" of the grass. We would give names to our baby grass and, in a motherly manner, tie it on our back with a single piece of cloth. We also went through the trash to retrieve the tomato and sardine cans that our mothers had thrown away. These were our pots to cook food for our imaginary husbands and family. We used clay mud to mold husbands and sons for ourselves.

I remember that we never had any tasks for our clay husbands except to eat the food we continuously prepared for them. However, we would quickly task our grass girls with cooking, cleaning and taking care of their siblings. Some girls had good skills in modeling the mud and could actually make something that would look like a human face. I remember that sometimes a girl would ask to share the "husband" of another playmate rather than mold her own clay. The borrower or "second wife" would then promise to respect and obey the "first wife". This was just an imitation of real life polygamy interactions. Girls of polygamist families were more likely to initiate this type of play arrangements.

I remember that I would run to the group of boys to see what kind of games they were playing, and I got beaten for it by my older brother for my curiosity. This happened almost every day.

I remember that after school, we girls had to go to the river to fetch drinking water, or to the garden to collect greens, then help in the kitchen and clean after dinner before we could go to play. When we would come home from school and our parents were gone, we would go straight to play until they returned, which would signal the beginning of chores and the end of games for that day.

I remember that each month, when the moon was full, we would go out to play with other kids late into the night. Sometimes we would walk to the next village and compete against the kids there to win small trophies such as food items, balls, dolls, etc. Girls would play against other girls, and boys would play against other boys. Some common games were jumping jacks, storytelling, dancing, singing and reciting Bible verses. Selected parents would accompany and chaperone us.

My Family
I am the third of six children and the second oldest girl in my family. I remember that my mother would often dress me in my brother's clothes. My father had died by the time I started elementary school, and left my brothers with more clothes than us girls, so my mother thought I should use some of their clothes. I was already wearing pants and shorts when I was only 6, a long time before the practice was accepted in the country. At first, I was mocked and bullied for that – my brother especially beat me a lot and led the charge in bullying me – but my mother insisted I had to take it or go naked. Besides, she said I looked better in pants than in skirts. Eventually I became known for dressing differently from most girls. I also learned progressively to fight back by adopting a passive aggressive behavior. I also learned to resist bullies and keep my cool when mocked.

I grew up in a Christian family. From the time we could speak, my mother would teach us short verses to repeat. We would first learn to pray before we ate, then we would learn Proverbs 6:22, then John 3:16, and so on. To this day, all of my mother's grandchildren and great-grandchildren know how to pray before they eat, and most have memorized at least one Bible verse. Christianity was the major religion in my country when I was growing up, and still is, although I believe to a lesser extent. However, I remember that most people in my neighborhood were following both a Christian religion and a traditional one. It was common to see people coming from church on Sunday and almost immediately set out to hold a pagan ceremony with incantations and other traditional rites.

I remember when I got baptized at age 8, my father was gravely ill at home and my mother was responsible for organizing the whole process. My older sister and I were baptized on the same day. My mother made us similar dresses in local African fabric. We call it *robes uniformes* in French. Along with us was another girl from the neighborhood. She was a little older and her name was Kobangue. Everybody suspected that she was a witch. They were looking at her in a funny way, and nobody wanted to come close to her. On the morning of the baptism, we got to the river by ourselves, but after the event we assembled by neighborhood groups and walked home together, with the newly baptized in the middle and everyone else forming a circle around them.

My mother shot me one of those looks, and I rushed over to hold Kobangue's hand as we marched home. The crowd around us was singing and stamping their feet all the way from the river to our homes, a good five miles away. The practice was to stop at the home of each of the newly baptized, starting with the one closest to the baptismal river. We would all stop briefly, pray for the person, eat or drink quickly what the family had to offer, and set off while that person and his or her family stayed, reducing the crowd each time. However, some new people joined as the group made its way to the next house.

As soon as we set out from the river on that Sunday in July, it started to rain heavily and people grumbled loudly, saying that this was the result of God pouring his anger over the unrepentant witch among us, because she was making light of the holiness of baptism. My mother assumed that people would not be inclined to accompany Kobangue to her home, which was the farthest out, so when we got to our home, she said, "My daughter Leonie has decided to combine her celebration with that of her new friend Kobangue. Please stay here and eat with us; there will not be a separate stop at Kobangue's house." And so it was. Leonie is my nickname. We shared our meal with Kobangue and all the well-wishers. Only later in the evening did my mother take my new friend home to her family. She was very grateful, she told me later. Afterwards, some strange things happened in the life of Kobangue, who was an adopted child. She became paralyzed from the waist down after an obscure household accident and was in a wheelchair for a decade. Then one Sunday when she was alone at the river doing her laundry, she heard a voice that told her to get up and walk. She did, and the whole neighborhood was astonished to see her walking home on her feet, having abandoned her wheelchair on the bank of the river. She officially converted to Christianity right then, because she believed the voice she heard was Jesus'. She frequently gave public testimonies in support of the Christian faith before she died a few years later.

My mother always wanted to follow the Bible literally, especially when it came to humility and charity. Our home was always open to the passersby. We welcomed strangers all the time, some staying as long as a year, and some making repetitive stops. Sometimes my mother would make us give up our beds and sleep on a mat next to her bed because there was one more stranger who needed a place to stay. I hated it because our beds were fitted with mosquito nets. When we slept on the floor, we would get mosquito bites and fever, but my mom could care less. She said God was protecting us. There was never a suspicion as to whether a stranger staying in our house might do us harm. There was no fear or concern for our safety and nothing bad happened either, except that occasionally someone would walk away with a wheelbarrow, some money, clothes or household items. My mother always insisted that God could protect us way better than anything we can do ourselves. She said, "If you start protecting yourself, God will wash His hands and let you do it your way, with all the consequences. But if you give God the task of protecting you, He will make it His business to assure that you are safe."

My father was an evangelist and church planter. We are told that my father was a young man, married and working as store manager for an expatriate businessman, when he was recruited by the American missionaries of the Baptist Mid Mission to work in evangelism. He was trained and sent to start churches in small villages around the country. He would stop in a village, gather a small group of volunteers, teach them the basics of the Bible, and teach them the habit of holding regular Bible meetings; then he would install a leader over the new church and move on to the next village. That's how he left his wife and young daughter behind and traveled up to my mother's village where he planted a new church, while at the same time working to earn my mom's hand. She was much younger, barely out of the circumcision camp. He married her and the missionaries fired him because they did not accept bigamy. However, my father never went back to his first wife. He divorced her when he could and shared custody of the girl. He never went back to live in the city where he was from. He continued to serve God as an evangelist for a non-missionary affiliated church.

My father died when I was 8 years old and my mother's oldest child was 12. My mother decided, according to her vow to my father and according to her faith, to remain a widow and devote her energy to raising her 7 children: two boys and five girls, including one stepdaughter. My father's family decided that my mother was being stubborn, so they took away from her most of the material goods that my father possessed. They left us the house nonetheless and, since we were still in the neighborhood, relatives of my father were always around. Some were nice and fed us or took care of us, while others were busy badmouthing my mother and us. My mother worked hard and, with the help of some church members and other good-willed people, was able to build up a nest of provision for our basic needs. I believe the church gave my mother a small allowance for at least a few years. She also worked as a day laborer on other people's farms.

We were not the richest family in the neighborhood, but definitely not the most disadvantaged either. We had a few head of goats, a few chickens, a vegetable garden and some basic things. We never went to bed hungry; there was always something to eat and share with people who were hungrier. However, it seemed weird and rude to bring food to school, and nobody was doing it, so I often felt hungry at school, especially in college where the school days lasted longer. The school was farther and I could no longer have mangos, since I was riding the bus back and forth rather than walking. Also, every day during my college years, when I got home from school, I had to cook for the visitors and my siblings, and then do my part of chores and bathe the little kids. Only after all this could I be allowed to eat and do my homework. It was during that period that I learned to go without food and to control my hunger. Much later on, this habit helped me with observing religious fasting.

Luckily for me, I started to earn a government allowance for good grades, and this made my mother happy. Each trimester I would bring home money to help with the expenses. I started to be my mother's sole financial partner, from that time up to now. She would tell me what her projects were and we would decide to set money aside little by little until we were able to get the project done. A few times my mother told me that she had used the money we'd been saving for Project A to do something else, such as giving to the church for a collection, or helping out a neighbor. I knew she didn't have to tell me anything, so I felt privileged she would confide in me, even though I felt disappointed.

From what my mother described, I believe my father died of bladder cancer, but I am not that sure. I decided very early on that I wanted to be a doctor. I wanted to understand diseases such as the one that killed my father. I found medicine to be very fascinating because you could do something to alleviate pain and suffering, with spectacular results sometimes. I wanted to be able to do that. I knew I could gain the knowledge to heal people. That's why I wanted to be a doctor. I wanted nothing else. I think I even conditioned myself so much that my mind became selective. I found myself better at understanding subject matters that were related to medicine (biology, math, physics) than subject matters that were not (philosophy, French literature). I was more interested in reading about the life of Pasteur than that of Victor Hugo, Albert Camus, or even Napoleon. I knew more about John Snow than I knew about the American agricultural system altogether, although that was a whole semester topic and most of my classmates were constantly talking about it.

My mother never discouraged me from my goal, but she insisted that my first priority be to become a good wife and a good mother. I remember that there was a Jehovah's Witness who lived nearby. He was regularly pacing the neighborhood and seeking to talk to people about his religion.

He must have been in his late forties when I was in high school. He liked to visit with me because I was among the few who could read the numerous brochures and other publications that he was always carrying. I liked his visits as well because his brochures usually included scientific analyses of social problems. Often he told me, "I have the revelation that you will serve as a bridge among several nations." He started to call me "meeting of nations." My mother and siblings used that to tease me whenever they were upset with me. They would call me "meeting of nations" to irritate me. My mother did not like that man. She did not like his religion, but she also did not like his false prophecy that I was to reunite nations. She said a good prophecy would have been to foretell that I would bear numerous children and make my husband and family proud, like in Proverbs 31. She made it a point to sit me down and warn me after each of his visits not to believe in false religions and false prophecies. However, she urged me to keep being nice to him because he was an elder. This was very confusing to me.

Cultural Conditioning

My mother was constantly monitoring my behavior to make sure that I never took credit for my intellectual abilities. Never, ever, as long as she lived. She said that it was God's hidden plan to give this or that ability to an individual one day or the other, and I was to be completely humble. I have learned to consistently check myself for any words or behaviors that might look like I am being proud of myself or immodest in any way. It was particularly hard because everything I said or did seemed to be interpreted as prideful and I was teased for it every single day. My brothers and sisters learned to shut me off by saying, "Yes, Miss Education." A lot of times I have wished I were not schooled at all. I have often wished that my brain would not breed all these ideas because I tend to immediately say out loud what comes to my mind.

On many occasions, I worked hard to "quiet" my mind and play dumb, so that I would belong and not appear more intellectual than others. After I was married, my husband would use the phrase *femme intellectuelle*, "educated woman," to shun me any time I said something smart or I seemed to challenge his dominant status in the household. One day, my husband was telling a joke and, before he could finish the story, I already knew what the joke would be. So I said it out loud without thinking. We were sitting in the courtyard with my brother, my children, and two sisters-in-law. My husband stopped talking, walked in the house and called me in. He gave me a few whips of his belt, put the belt back on, and walked out with only two words: *femme intellectuelle*. I cried softly but then he called me outside again, so I quickly washed my face, put on some lotion and came out smiling. I wish it had stopped there, but it did not. I ran into troubles too many times for voicing what came through my brain. I am still learning to think more and say less. Now I am at a point where I always talk when I shouldn't open my mouth, and I keep quiet when I should speak out. It is so frustrating!

I grew up in the seventies, which was the most peaceful period in the history of my country. In 1966, General Bokassa of the national army forces successfully led a coup d'état to oust the president at the time, who was his own young cousin. By 1970, he had established himself as an uncontested leader and a world renowned dictator, having moved to systematically and radically eliminate all real or suspected dissidents, sometimes decimating entire families. He was rumored to be a cannibal since many of his enemies, especially the staunchest or most outspoken ones, would simply vanish without a trace. In the seventies, President Bokassa implemented policies to improve the economic status of the country. He created the first university, built roads and established a national cooperative for agricultural development and food self-sufficiency. Only people who had political ambitions were insecure or fearful. The rest of the population was pretty safe.

There were numerous occasions where the president decreed on a whim that the people should celebrate and be glad. For example, each time his wife gave birth he would go on the national radio and declare a national holiday. Once he described his newborn boy as having six fingers on each hand and six toes on each foot, which was a distinct familial trait. Therefore, he said, we would have two days of national holiday. The treasury secretary was urged to work overnight to pay salaries so that people could celebrate. Every government employee was ordered to get up that night and go downtown to receive their pay before dawn. For those outside of the capital, each province administrator was ordered to take money wherever they could and pay salaries starting at daybreak, because the provinces generally did not have electricity to work overnight. Provinces would start their forty-eight hour holiday a half day later than people in the capital. Since the government was the single biggest employer in the country, most people got paid and were urged to use the money to drink and celebrate the birth of the president's son. Breweries and major grocery stores were ordered to work overtime and employers were ordered to give double pay to the employees who needed to be at work. Private employers also paid their employees in advance and gave them a two-day paid holiday, so that they would not appear as dissidents to the president. Very frequently, when salaries were not paid for several months, public servants and other government employees would start circulating the rumor that the president's wife was in her second trimester of pregnancy and salaries were being held until she gave birth.

In 1977, the president crowned himself emperor, in the image of Napoleon and the Shah of Iran, he said. He declared that the country would become an empire. A big celebration was organized with parades, traditional dances and other ceremonies. Around the country, every woman who had six children or more was given a medal: bronze for 6-7 children, silver for 8-9 children, and gold for mothers with 10 or more children. The awards also included a small amount of money designed to pay for family celebrations. My mother had 6 children, so she was a bronze medal recipient. I don't know how much money she received. She does not remember.

The emperor also decreed that Mother's Day would be a major holiday, second only to the celebration of Saint Sylvester Day, the day he ascended to power. On Mother's Day (the last Sunday in May or the first Sunday in June, if May ends closer to a weekend), the Emperor always spoke on the radio, urging men to honor the mothers of their children and suggesting that they seek and marry a woman that could bear them a number of children worthy of a medal. To this day, Mother's Day is a major holiday in the country, now second only to Christmas.

Education

Girls were free to go to school, only we were supposed to be good wives and good mothers first. We went to school to be able to write letters for our elders and maybe read the Bible. We also went to school to learn sewing and housekeeping. Catholic schools for girls put a strong emphasis on these subject matters. I could have quit school anytime, and it would have been just fine. Several times I found myself missing notebooks and other school supplies. My mother used my notebooks to wrap merchandise for her customers. Sometimes she gave away my school books, especially the science and other colorful books, to other children who used them as toys. Thinking back, I still wonder how I was able to succeed with all these setbacks. I can remember that only a few of my classmates finished high school. And many of them probably had more supportive parents.

I went to an all girls' catholic elementary school called Sainte Monique. It was next door to an all boys' catholic school called Saint Pierre. The two were separated by tall, wired fences. I remember that in the 5th and 6th grades my teacher was also the paternal uncle of one of my classmates, Jacqueline. The teacher wanted Jacqueline to succeed so much. He always told her something like, "I want you to be smart like Leonie. In today's life you need to be educated." He liked me a lot and often referred to me as his favorite student. He would come to our home each month to report to my mother about my grades and my behavior. I don't think my mother cared much about the grades, but she always cooked food and prepared a Bible verse to share with him when he would come. The teacher beat Jacqueline more often and harder than any other student. He punished her severely for every small mistake. But Jacqueline was very good-hearted. She was one of my best friends. She asked me to go over the assignments with her during recess. She asked what my secret was for getting all these good grades. I responded honestly that I did not have a secret – I just had a very good memory.

In class, I was a very serious student, keeping quiet and hanging onto every word the teacher uttered. After school, I never got the time to do anything school-related: I had chores to attend to and visitors to help take care of. My older siblings were not that interested in school to want to help me. My mother was just neutral, and she never missed an opportunity to throw away the school books to make room for things she valued more. Every now and then, I would find a way to sneak into the boys' room, where my brother and his friends discussed their homework in between games. The room was furnished with a blackboard and pieces of chalk. I would listen and take in everything I could until my mother came or called me, or until my brother got frustrated and took it out on me by kicking and hitting me out of the room.

I completed my homework assignments at night or early in the morning because I always got to school before class started. I loved school because it was easy for me – I had good grades, the teachers loved me, and I got frequent rewards from the catholic nuns like candies, dolls and other toys that I could share with my friends. At times, I bribed my brother with my candies so he would let me stay in the boys' homework room. When I was circumcised, I confessed to that behavior at the initiation camp. I was flogged and told not to go to the boys' room anymore, so I didn't. Well, maybe I did by habit a couple of times, but then I quit completely.

I relied heavily on auditory teaching and my learning style was based on direct interaction with the teachers. This has played a role in some of the failures in my life. During my last year of college, I got married and became pregnant. I was constantly tired and I slept a lot during class. I could not hear everything the teachers were saying. In fact, sometimes my drowsy state led me to memorize a twisted version of the teachers' statements. I was putting statements on my paper that the teachers denied they ever made. By that time, I had become somewhat confident about my intelligence, so I would take the unusual step of challenging teachers about my grades. I would go to the teacher and say, "I heard you say this in class. Why did you strike it when I repeated it on my paper?" and they would say, "You misunderstood. I did not say this. Rather, I said that." After a few incidents, I concluded I must be mixing what the teachers said with my own dreams.

I also started to miss classes, because I had frequent urinary tract infections and my husband insisted that I go to the clinic for treatment, to protect the unborn baby. I had rarely missed school at all, from the day I was enrolled in kindergarten until that year. Even though I had classmates that let me copy their notes, I could not catch up because I needed to hear the lecture myself to better memorize it. My grades suffered greatly.

My high school principal was one of the few people who really believed in me. A few years after I went to college, he was promoted to national director in the Department of Education. I believe he placed a call to the dean of my college to check on my progress. He was distraught when the dean told him that my grades were not good. One day, the dean went from classroom to classroom to introduce his boss, the new director of education. They came to my classroom and there I was in the front row, looking very pregnant as I came face-to-face with my high school principal for the first time in 4 years. He did not say anything to me but I knew he was disappointed. That day I also knew that he could have helped me if I had gone to him with the issue of my arranged marriage. But part of me reasoned it was too late, and besides, what could he have done?

I barely made the passing score for the Bachelor's degree. As is the practice, the names of the graduates were read on the radio. Every family that had a student who took the test was gathered around their radio to follow the readings but my family did not waste their time. A classmate of mine took it upon herself to walk to my house and announce the news to me. Then a few other people told us they heard my name. That was it. One week after the results were announced, I gave birth to my first child, a girl. Everybody was talking about my new baby and how she looked like her father, but nobody thought about congratulating me for my Bachelor's degree. My mother-in-law even suggested that if I had stayed put instead of acting restless because of school issues, I would have had a boy. She said boys are a fearful and very private gender. They come only to mothers that are quiet and gentle. She said I always acted too rough to bear a boy.

The custom in my country was that college graduates have to take an exam called *test psychotechnique* to help match them with the appropriate graduate program. The test took a whole day and parts of it looked a lot like an IQ test. When I was scheduled for the interview and disclosure of my test results, the official told me, "You said on the test that you wanted to be a doctor. Is that right?" I said, "Yes." He asked, "Are you married?" I said, "Yes." I also said that I had just had a baby girl.

The scheduler said, "You have scored equally well in math, science and literature. I give you two very good options to choose from: you can go to the *école normale* and be a teacher after two short years of training. You can choose to teach math or science. We need more math teachers than language and literature teachers, you know. Or you can go to the agricultural school in M'baiki (the town where it's located, about seventy miles from the capital city) and become an agricultural technician in three years. I believe your husband would oppose that option." So he scheduled me to take the normal school entrance exam in two weeks' time. This was sometime in August and school was to start October 1st.

The following Monday, early in the morning, I put on my nicest dress and showed up at the government office building downtown. I looked up the office of the director of education and stood at the door waiting. I did not want to sit in the waiting room, since I did not have an appointment. Finally, my high school principal, now the director of education, arrived. As soon as he saw me, he handed his briefcase and walkie-talkie to one of his aides, swept me off my feet, spun me around and kissed me on both cheeks. Then he took me by the hand and led me to his desk to talk. I told him I had given birth, and told him whom I was married to. He knew all about the results of the psychotechnical exam, and my application for normal school. He had secretly hoped I would stick to my guns. He asked me only, "Do you still want to be a doctor?" I said, "Yes sir." "Are you sure?" I said, "Yes, yes sir." He called his secretary and said, "Stephanie (I am not sure I remember her name correctly), may I introduce to you Doctor …? Help her with her paperwork before you do anything else today." That's how I got into medical school.

My husband was beside himself. After the beating and intense questioning, I confessed to him that my mentor and high school principal helped me. We both went to see the principal, again without any appointment. In Africa you never go to see a high government employee without an appointment but we met him at his door. He had us wait a little, then took us to his car and drove us to his house for an impromptu brunch together. I stayed with his wife in the backyard while he and my husband talked for a few minutes inside. On the way home, my husband said, "As you wish, intellectual woman." And the rest is history. I received a few beatings and endured maybe two weeks of silent treatment, but we never talked about this again. In fact, he grew to like it because he would proudly tell his family to come to me with any ailments, aches or pains. Besides, with my long hours of internship in the hospital, he was happy to do what he wanted with other women. Each time I caught him with a woman was when I returned home unexpectedly.

Medical School
Medical school was tough. I had children to bring up, in-laws to deal with and my own family was disintegrating fast. I could barely take it. Several times, I was on the brink of a mental breakdown. I was easily distracted in school and could not concentrate. I also developed a stomach ulcer that

would send me crawling on the floor with pain. Adding to that were my frequent urinary infections. I was a wreck. I was a miserable wreck.

It was almost impossible for me to meet the needs of my mother and my husband at the same time. When I got married, I moved in with my husband to a house several miles away. Because of school and my kids, I could not see my mother often; sometimes I would go two full months without visiting with her. We did not have a telephone to communicate. Also, every time I wanted to go visit my mother, my husband insisted that we go together. We would visit my mother together, then his mother, and come back. Therefore, we needed to plan a whole afternoon for that, and coordinate with the caretakers for my kids. It was hard.

Although my mother was happy to see me go into marriage, she quickly became irritated by this type of arrangement. We did not have any more privacy to talk about our common projects, and I did not have any more freedom to give her all my money. My husband now decided what amount to give to my mother and when. Generally, he would insist that we give the same amount to my mother-in-law as well, which I thought was unfair. My mother-in-law had a husband and five out of six sons who had jobs and were earning money. My mother had only me.

On a few occasions when we visited my mother I would ask my husband ahead of time if I could stay longer so my mother could braid my hair. Even then, my husband would pull a chair and sit right by me while my mother was working on my head for two to three hours. I could feel my mother's hand tighten with frustration; her eyes would mist and she would wipe them frequently, explaining that she was getting old and her eyes were tiring easy. I knew she was crying about not being able to have the closeness we used to share. I cried a lot too about that.

I often argued with my husband about helping my mother out financially. He refused and sometimes I would take a beating for nagging him. He insisted that my mother was misusing the money. Three of my four sisters married into polygamist households and often relied on my mother for provisions; my two brothers became alcoholics and absentee fathers, so my mother gladly took in their children and occasionally had to cater to my brothers' drinking buddies as well. She nonetheless insisted on hosting strangers and feeding hungry people. My mother's strength was dwindling, so she could no longer do farm work for hire. She used up the few chickens and goats that she had, and some were stolen, I suspect, by my brothers for alcohol money. Every time I ran into people from my mother's neighborhood, they would tell me, "Your mother's been very sad since you left her." I felt guilty about that for a long time.

I started to take money from the grocery allowance and hide it. Then I would give it to people who could take it to my mother. I also stole items from our food pantry to send to my mother when my husband was not watching. I rationalized it by saying to myself, "I also contribute to the general finances of this house so I have some right to take from them. Besides, I don't know what my husband does with the rest of the money, which also includes my contribution." However, sometimes I felt so guilty that I would decide to forego a meal or two as my own restitution for what I had taken for my mother.

My husband was very consistent in buying me gold jewelry for each anniversary. A few times I sold my gold jewelry and told my husband that it was stolen at the student lounge in the hospital. I sent the money to my mother.

After my third year in medical school, I started to substitute teach for some of my professors at the school of nursing and the Red Cross. I told my husband I was on call. I told my professors to give the honoraria directly to my mother.

My mother and I got a break when I went for my residency training. We had to spend a full year in the countryside to train in rural health. I was there with my two girls and my younger sister. My husband visited every trimester. There, I was free to set provisions aside for my mother. She even visited me and stayed for two full months. During that visit, she and I started making plans for me to build a small house near her, just in case. We consulted with my best friend Vickie to act as the go-between. Vickie would visit me once or twice a month to collect whatever amount I could muster, and take it to my mother for the project. It took us several years, and Vickie moved with her husband to a different city in the meantime, but we were able to finish the project anyway.

The country went through a series of political upheavals throughout the eighties, and schools were often closed, but hospitals remained open. As medical students, we were always expected to dodge the bullets and show up for clinical rotations. Sometimes I got stranded in the hospital and had to spend the night and the next day I would have to finish my regular round and schedule before I could go home. I feared for my children while I was away. When I was home with my kids, I feared for my mother. Yet I was determined to earn my degree, and I was glad I accomplished it.

I did my thesis on the assessment of the eight elements of primary health care in a selected community. When I was defending my thesis, I was so focused on the slide projector and my presentation, that I did not pay attention to the people entering the room. It was relatively crowded. I was very happily surprised to see my high school principal (and number one fan) at the end of the event coming from the back of the room with a small entourage. He said, "Dr ...." And I said, "Sir." He said, "No, call me Etienne." I said, "Yes sir, I will." Of course he lifted me up and whirled me around to congratulate me. That was the proudest moment of my life.

Some years later, I ran into him again. He told me, "I just came back from New York. I wish for you one day to be able to visit America. Once you get there you'll understand why I say that." When I came to the USA I heard of him twice. The first time, my mother mentioned during a phone conversation that he had stopped at the house to inquire about my whereabouts. I sent him a few postcards to thank him for his mentorship, guidance and friendship. I said I was starting to understand why he wanted for me to come to America. I will never know whether he got them, given how unreliable the postal service is in my country. The second time I heard of him, my mother again mentioned during a conversation that he had died. I cried and cried and cried again. I miss him so much. I still dream about him regularly – when I am facing a difficult decision and I wish that someone would advise and guide me, I see him in a dream shortly afterwards. However, he barely talks to me in my dreams, so I think I will have to do without his advice forever now.

Circumcision Camp

While my childhood was mostly happy, it was a different story when I reached adolescence. When I came back from the circumcision camp, things were never the same again. We had transitioned from girlhood to womanhood when we returned. Therefore, we were harshly warned against playing with other girls if they were not circumcised. We were told to consider ourselves more emancipated, having been initiated to womanly virtues and character.

Marianne was kind of my protégé; she was a little younger, I believe. My mother had said that I was a few months younger than Marianne but I did not believe her, since Marianne was smaller and shorter than I was. Besides, I needed someone to rule over, and Marianne assumed the role perfectly. She was a good imitator and a good listener. She followed and I led. I convinced Marianne to go with me through circumcision, so that we could continue to play together and share secrets once we returned. Unfortunately, she never made it out, so I felt (and still feel) guilty for her loss.

We prepared frantically for the camp. We had seen the girls that had gone to camp and returned. They were more valued than their peers and they married quickly afterwards. Their parents were respected. My mother told us that we would be going during the next cycle. We were to keep it a secret but I told my friends and I asked them to go with me so we could "emancipate" together. Marianne was really the only one that came with me. Two of my friends (Aimée and her sister Elizabeth) went to a different camp because they belonged to a different tribe and their initiation process was not exactly the same. Plus, they went to camp before we did, even though we were of the same age. When Aimée and Elie came back from initiation, they continued to play with me because they knew I would be going to camp as well. But I did not go until maybe two or three years later.

Throughout the school year, we prepared for the big event that was set to take place during summer vacation. We saved money, bought articles of beauty and jewelry and hid them. My mother made us a couple of similar dresses: one to go out in, and one to wear on the big day of return. On the last day of school, we could not wait to pack our belongings and go to camp. It was like finally being able to join an exclusive club.

My mother made the arrangements with the people who organized the camp. I don't know how much she paid or who was paid. All I know is that my sister and I had the same chaperone. She was primarily responsible for assuring that we learned what we needed to learn, and she checked on us every day to see how our healing process was coming along. Also, when we did something wrong, they would call her to report to her and she always participated in deciding what punishment we were to receive. When my mother sent food or greetings, she was the one who decided whether we should be informed or not. I say this because after we got home, my mother asked how many times we had received special treats and messages from her. My sister and I counted on our fingers, and we saw that my mother was not happy with the total number. However, she did not elaborate, and we did not ask, since we knew better to never question our initiators.

On the day we left for camp, each of us packed our personal belongings and came out on the street around midday. We stood in a single line according to our height. One older lady appeared that I had not met before. She led us along with other women from the neighborhood. We were about ten to fifteen girls, aged six to fourteen. I was barely ten years old and my sister was fourteen. We were much older than the other girls, maybe because we were going to school full time; because my father had died and, as a single parent, my mother needed more time to gather the needed amount; or just because my mother had been initially hesitant about sending us to camp, being that she was a pious Christian.

We started with enthusiasm – singing, clapping with our loads balanced on top of our heads, and tapping our feet to the cadence. But soon some of us started to feel tired. First, I stopped clapping. Then, I stopped singing after a while. Then, I started lagging behind the group, prompting the chaperones to hit and push me. So I started crying. I was not alone though – several girls did the same before or after me. It was a long walk. When we arrived at the destination, the sun had set and it was getting dark.

There were people there waiting for us. They told us to put our belongings on the dirt floor of the tents. We were separated into small groups, given food to eat and quickly sent to bed. We slept on traditional mats, cramped together. There was a wood fire burning, with the smoke filling the tents, and the chaperones were sitting by the fire and talking all night. I was afraid and nervous at the same time.

Very early in the morning, we were awakened with the loud sound of a whistle. They told us to strip out of our clothes. Then they arranged us again in one line according to height and we departed for the operating location farther into the bush, near the river. Once there, we lay down on mats of banana leaves, as they told us. We were told to lie face up and cover our face with our hands. The chaperones were checking and if we opened our eyes they would pour pepper sauce in them. It was forbidden for us to speak so after a while some girls fell asleep.

The older lady from the previous day took a tour to check the size of our organs, and then she went to her seat. She was seated on a small mound with a sort of operating table made of layers of wild leaves set out before her. There was a row of leaf mats on each side of her. The two chaperones would take us, one at a time, to the table where the operator was. Once we were operated on, we were transported to the other side to lay and wait until everybody was cut.

Marianne was smaller, so she went before me. I think I must have dozed off; I did not see her being led out. I would never see her again. When it was my turn, my chaperone took my hand and led me to the older lady. I was told to open my legs as wide as I could. The older lady was seated right between my legs and already parting my limbs with her own thighs. One chaperone knelt on one side of my head, and another on the other side. They grabbed whatever part of my body seemed to be moving, and held me with their weight and strength to assure that I was completely restrained. My only concern was to be sure I could breathe, as my mother had taught us. She said, "Move if you can't breathe, but once your nose has access to air, freeze." I saw the old lady's bloody little blade going between my legs, then felt a sharp pain, lasting maybe 5 seconds, that seemed like eternity. She then applied some pressure, checked and cut some edges. It was very, very painful this time. Then she applied pressure again and checked. She told the chaperones, "She is good," and they carried me to the next row of girls, put me on a mat, tied my legs with some wild rope and put a piece of fabric over me. I cried for a while, and then fell asleep. I slept in short episodes, interrupted by the pain and the weird feeling of blood between my legs. When it was finished, they made us stand up and walk back to camp. Very painful, the friction of your legs together. Until then, I did not realize that my inner thighs touched when I walked. But still, this was nothing compared to the burning pain I felt when I first urinated after the operation. I learned to drink less and avoid going to the bathroom if I could help it. We cried. Almost everybody cried, and they whipped us good. One cousin was very stoic; she kind of laughed out loud when the rest of us cried. They whipped her as well, saying that she was not giving respect to the tradition.

When we arrived in camp, we were assigned to small groups each with a group leader. That's where I first got to talk and I asked where Marianne was. I was told that she would not be joining us that day, that she was coming later. They gave us special clothes: pieces of fabric sewn as loose slips with adjusting ropes. We wore the slips around our chest and the adjusting rope that came out of the slip edge was tied behind our neck. It was very uncomfortable. The leaders had their own headquarters where they made the deliberations, and where they stocked all the goods that would sustain us during the six weeks. They fed us bitter leaves and wild yams.

That same evening, we were led out to the river for our first wash. The chaperones held my legs apart and lowered me so that the water current was hitting my wounds with an optimum force. This washed away the clots but also opened new blood vessels. So when we got back to camp, I had blood running down to my feet and sticking to my dress. I slept with the smell of blood and the sandy feeling of blood particles between my legs. After two days, however, my wound was dry and I could even run and play with my campmates. Only then did I allow myself to go to the bathroom a second time.

We learned a lot of skills during the time we were at camp. We learned to work in groups, to trust one another, to fish, to survive in the wilderness. We also learned to serve and obey our husbands. We learned to take care of our children. The way we learned those things was mostly by riddles. They would send a group out with a few clues and tell them to reach a desired outcome. Any failure would lead to physical punishment. Lack of teamwork would lead to double punishment for each member. What's more, they never told us exactly what we did wrong. They would keep beating us until we figured out what was wrong and changed course.

My sister and I devised a way to help each other out. When I was in trouble, my sister would come with another campmate within earshot of me. She would then talk to the campmate in codes for me to hear. I did the same for her whenever I could although I don't think I helped much because I was not as perceptive. One day, it was my group's turn to cook. So I was sent out with another girl to fetch water. I followed her to the river, filled my pot and followed her back. Although I was visibly older, the forest was not my kind of environment, so I let her go first. When we got back, they whipped me but not her.

After the beating, they told me to join another girl to get firewood. I followed her back with my small fagot, and they whipped me again. While I was crying, I saw my sister playing a game with her friend. She said, "Today I call you chipmunk, chipmunk that's you." That was my clue. After they whipped me for the second time, they withheld my lunch and later sent me out with two more girls to get wild yams for dinner. I knew that if I missed that time, I would go to bed hungry, after another round of beating.

As soon as we set out, I went my own way and joined the group only when it was time to come back to camp. That's how I passed the trial. They wanted me to prove that I could do things on my own while belonging to the group. In the first two attempts, I had been following my teammates. So when my sister said, "chipmunk," I thought about the story of the chipmunk that my mother told us. The chipmunk was an imitator. He wanted to imitate the rat and got burnt in the process. The lesson of the chipmunk story was: *don't always follow. Sometimes you need to break away from the group and do things on your own.*

We also had personal times with the leaders where we were asked to confess any weaknesses or bad habits. After deliberation they would tell us what the penalty for our faults would be. It was mostly whipping, withholding meals or organized mocking sessions where everybody ridiculed and derided you until you broke down. There was not a single girl who had not received a severe beating, to the point of bleeding. Several girls were hurt more than I was. And I was whipped there more than any other time in my life. I found out there that the daily beatings I had taken from my brother were mere scratches.

After about six weeks in the bush and after most of us had healed, we were told one evening that in two days we would be ready to go home. So, on the eve of our return, I had my last appearance before the leaders. Only after fighting hard with me did they get to see my wounds, so they congratulated me for passing that test. They told me that I did well with completing the penalties for my transgressions and bad habits. They told me that I was going to be a good wife and that my future in-laws had been notified of my progress and good behavior. I took an oath to respect all the camp leaders forever, to keep secret the things I had seen or heard in camp, and to be forever loyal to the tradition when I had my own daughters.

On the return day, we discarded our camp attire, which went to the older lady's collection. We put on our nice dresses and underwear for the first time. It felt different; a little awkward at first. We took one last oath as a group to love one another unconditionally and keep one another's secrets; and we left.

Once we came close to home we started singing and clapping. Several people in the neighborhood came to meet us and walk home with us. My future husband's family came in a group to welcome me. His mother put a necklace around my neck and some of his relatives broke through the crowd to seek me out, kiss me and hug me. That's how I knew that I would be married to a boy from that family – I just didn't know which one. His mother had six sons, and only one was younger than me. Any of the other five could be the one they had chosen for me, even the older one who was already married. So I started reviewing the five sons in my head, and I prayed that the family had picked someone I could also like.

When we did not see Marianne join us in the camp, we started speculating. Some said they pulled her out because her parents did not pay the fees; others said that her mother, who drinks a lot of local alcohol, wanted to take her home and treat her wounds with alcohol which, after all, was better than the natural water we used in the camp; still others said she was so skinny she needed to be treated in the hospital, lest her wounds would not heal. But when we returned home, Marianne was still not there. Her mother came to meet us about three miles out. She stayed behind and did not come close to the group. I didn't know why. Once we got home she came and visited with me, even before my mother had private time with me. She told me that Marianne had died. She said they rushed her to the hospital because she was still bleeding one full day after the cutting. She said Marianne had lost consciousness when she got to the hospital. She never got to talk to her. We cried together. My mother and sister joined us and we cried for a long time. I'll never forget that. I secretly made a promise to myself to provide support to Marianne's mother every time I could.

I went to camp to become emancipated. I convinced my friend to go with me so we could pass this step together on our way to a lifelong friendship. Instead I came out with a body riddled with scars and a deep resentment for the way things were taught there. I acquired difficulties with passing urine and learned haunting secrets that I would have been better off not knowing. I was pre-marked to be married to a man that I might not like and, most of all, I lost my good friend. The whole experience seemed very wrong and my return day turned into a very bitter day. I probably never regained my joyful nature after that.

My sister was also betrothed to a boy in the neighborhood. His name was Jacques (James). She liked him. Jacques was one of our playmates before we went to camp. He helped us win against boys from rival neighborhoods. So my sister was happy when Jacques' parents sent word to reserve her hand for him. In the camp, we had learned that some of the girls were not actually virgins. We learned that they were found to have a "hole." My sister decided, "Hole or no hole, you get the same whipping with this damn initiation." Besides, at fourteen she was too old to continue waiting. So she and Jacques took the game to the next level. I don't know if the parents on either side were aware of that or not. In any case, Jacques died in a car accident less than a year later, way before his parents could organize the wedding. She went on to marry the next man whose family also wanted her for him. He was much older with two wives already. She bore six children, ran away several times, and shared her husband with two older women before finally divorcing him to marry someone of her own choosing.

Several girls from our initiation group went on to be chronically depressed or addicted to alcohol. One, by the name Angele, suffered from what I now suspect to be schizophrenia. She would talk to people we could not see, obey voices only in her head, and she became scared to the point of being violent if approached.

My only tangible lasting effects are the recurrent urinary infections I have gotten through the years. After the initiation, I talked to my mother often about the bad dreams, the fears, the infections, and the disillusionment I had. Most of the time she would listen intently, then say, "You'll survive, I promise. Who knew I would live to see a fine woman like you, let alone give birth to a fine woman like you?" And she would smile. My interpretation was that maybe she had suffered even more than we did. "But why didn't you protect us?" I would ask. She would respond, "Only God can protect you. He is doing just that. I am glad he is doing that".

Womanhood
My husband was the third oldest, just like me. He was just out of the seminary and wanted to get married. He insisted on having a schooled wife to whom he could write, since he was away in school and had been for several years. You see, he was adopted by some French missionaries and enrolled in a Jesuit seminary abroad. But he decided to drop out and wanted to come home to his biological family. The priests insisted that he

at least continue on to civilian education, while his parents were searching for a wife for him to marry. All his school needs were met by the Jesuit Brotherhood. The priests liked the description of me that was sent on by his parents; I believe they helped financially. When I saw him (as such) for the first time, it was almost five years after I got back from my initiation. I was, however, shown a picture of him after I had completed enough requirements to win more of his family's trust. He did not begin to write to me until after we had met and married.

Meanwhile, I continued to go to school as usual. The only problem was, I had two families to work for. I still had my chores and other duties in my original household. Additionally, I now belonged to the family of my future husband, so they wanted to know what I was capable of accomplishing as a wife. His relatives would call on me to go fetch water for them, cook for them, do grocery shopping, write or read letters for them – all kinds of things.

They also checked on me often to make sure that I was well-behaved. They paid a respected lady in the neighborhood to check on my virginity. Every month, the lady would come. She would meet with my mother and my future mother-in-law. They would say, "Go wash and come back. It's time." So I would quickly splash my parts to clean off any urine drops, take off my undies, come back and lie down. They would part my legs and each of them would check: first Auntie Lucia, then my mother-in-law, then my mother. They would look, touch, and say, "Just as we saw last month; still good." I'd wait until all three agreed; then I'd get up and get dressed. My mother felt especially proud and happy after these sessions. Several times, my mother-in-law requested that I be checked out between sessions because she said she had heard rumors. She would tell my mother, "Let's just do it, you and me, and if we see something suspicious, I will call Lucia."

When I got my period, it was a big catastrophe because the conventional wisdom was that virgins could not possibly "see the moon," as we call it. We were taught in camp that we should be "tight" with no hole for blood to come out. You get your period when you have been with a man and he has opened the way for blood to flow out. Girls who showed holes after the circumcision were suspected of being "loose" and referred to be sewn further. I was still a virgin when I got my first period. But again, I was not your typical girl. All my campmates had become mothers by the time I got married, although I was much older than most of them when we went to camp. My mother knew I was a virgin. Yet, I knew what she believed with regard to first menstruations. I could not tell her. We never discussed these kinds of things. I could not ask my sister. She had so many problems of her own that I doubted she could keep a secret. I suspected she would use this information as a chip to try to extort her freedom or some other concession from my mother or her family-in-law. I had to hide it. But how could I? I had a heavy flow right on my first cycle; blood smells, and blood stains. Additionally, the way our communities were set up, the washrooms were usually located at the far end of the properties. When we went to wash, we would carry a bucket of water across the yard to the washroom. So if you carried a bucket to the bathroom three to four times a day, people would notice and start to talk. And your mother-in-law-to-be would certainly order a check-up. I was mortified. It was a very messy few days. It was humiliating. Not just that first cycle, but other cycles after that as well. Not just at home, but at school as well.

It was one of the most traumatic times in my life. I had not completely recovered from the shock of the camp yet and this happened. I hated my body. I hated that part of my humanness. If I had loved being a girl, I hated being a woman ten times more. I hated my life. I just hated it.

I survived, as my mother said, and I got married. My husband came home from Cameroon a week before the wedding, and he was set to go on to Germany shortly after. He was eight years older than me and we were born on the same day. He was well educated, I was told. I found him to be overbearing, a stranger, not as nice looking as in the picture. I did not know how to relate to him. I thought to myself, "This will take a lot of getting used to." I had a lot of ideas floating in my mind at the same time: a sense of excitement because I had accomplished what was expected of me, and a sense of failure and guilt and oppression. I said to myself, "If this is all life has to offer, it is not worth it." I was basically tired of life as I knew it. I wanted to revolt against something, anything. I hated to continue living the way I was. I wanted a change.

My husband, however, seemed happy with what he got. After the traditional marriage, he quickly organized a civil wedding at city hall. Right there at the altar he declared that he wanted me to be his only wife. That declaration surprised his mother, and she referred to it very often when my first child turned out to be a girl. You see, in my country men are allowed to marry up to four wives. I have seen cases where a man would go to the city hall with two or three women and marry them all during a single ceremony. When performing a wedding, the officer always asks the husband of his intentions. If he says it is a monogamous marriage, he has to pay supplemental fees for the declaration to be registered and written on the marriage certificate. Only in those cases can the wife legitimately divorce her husband if he decides later on to marry another woman. However, mistresses do not count; therefore a man can be in a monogamous marriage and still have as many mistresses as he wants or can afford. He just cannot be married to two women at the same time. We had not discussed the topic beforehand, so I was glad that my husband valued me enough to do that. But as I would learn later, the catholic group that was sponsoring my husband made it clear that he could not have more than one wife and still receive their support.

Married Life

After I got married, my family responsibilities increased with the birth of my children. My responsibility to my mother's household increased because my siblings were also beginning to have children and I needed to help my mother care for my siblings and their children. My responsibilities in school increased when I entered medical school.

My life was quite unusual. I was initiated and betrothed at ten, but I did not marry until I was fifteen. Two days after my marriage, my husband returned to Europe and I didn't see him until about one year later. I continued going to school and nursing my six-month-old niece when my sister ran away after being battered by both of her co-spouses. She went into hiding for about nine months. My mother said that I was long past due in becoming a mother, and this was my chance to at least practice being one. Besides, the girl would be better off with me than with either of her father's wives. So I took her with me. I would have the girl suck my small breasts whenever she cried; plus, I was given some herbs to drink, so after a few days I started to produce milk.

I remember how my husband hated that move. He was still in training in Germany when that happened. One day, on his way to Brazzaville for a conference, he made a stop to surprise me. As soon as he arrived he dropped his suitcase on the ground, grabbed me by the elbow and wanted to pull me inside. I resisted and said, "I am currently having my period. Besides, I am still nursing the baby and she is sleeping in the bed inside." He ground his teeth, made a fist and hit the wall repeatedly, mumbled about wasting everything or something like that. Then he picked up his suitcase and left. I called after him and offered for him to sit and eat something, or at least take a shower. He was gone. I learned later that he stayed for two days before departing.

My sister never really bonded with that girl, which I continued to nurse until the age of about fifteen months. Only later, at age seven, did the girl learn that I was actually her "little mother" or Auntie. All her life, she had considered me to be her mother and we had a closer relationship than the one she had with my sister. My in-laws had given up hope and were already talking about getting another wife for my husband, so that he might have a child before they died. I did not bear my first child until I was eighteen.

My husband wanted me to be the perfect wife: a completely independent woman when it came to keeping the house, yet a completely submissive woman when it came to making decisions and spending money. We argued often. I felt crushed, I felt bullied. I had been bullied a lot by my brother growing up, so I resented my husband even more when he ridiculed me into submitting to his will.

I was unhappy in my early adult life. I was restless and angry. I started to join student marches and teachers who were picketing for their salaries. I felt close to underdog groups. I felt like I understood the problems of oppressed groups everywhere.

I resented that my husband was allowed to control my schedule in school. I was upset that he had easier access to the dean in my school than I did. I hated that he would beat me up for the smallest thing. First my brother, then my initiators, and now my husband. I resented that he and his family or friends knew about every move I made, and yet I didn't know how he spent his days. I did not like it that each time people talked to me they started with "if your husband agrees…" or "if it's OK with your husband…" Even my teachers! Even my family! I was miserable. I cried a lot – I still can't remember a day during my marriage when I did not shed a tear.

Career
In medical school, I learned a lot of truth about the female anatomy and physiology. I started discussions with my male classmates about the potential consequences of the operation that I had. I learned that what my Aunt Valentine had could have been a complication of pregnancy. Aunt Valentine (a cousin of my father's) had difficulties with her first baby's delivery. They had to cut her to make way for the baby. Shortly after that she lost control of her bladder. Her husband took the baby away, gave it to his other wife to raise and threw my aunt out. So now she was going from house to house to beg for food and a place to stay. But she could not stay long with anybody because she always smelled like urine, and her clothes were always damp. Flies would converge wherever she went. So whenever she approached a relative's house, they would close their door and pretend that they were not home. She stayed with us on several occasions but only for a few days at a time, because then my mother would get exasperated and she would say, "Valentine, please go to such and such for a while, and then you can come back here. We just cannot have you indefinitely." Aunt Valentine was very understanding and very humble. She would say goodbye, wander around, and come again a few days later. When she died of infection, hunger, and maybe other things, we did not see the husband or even her daughter once during the whole month of funeral.

During clinical rotations I met many women in my Aunt Valentine's situation. I loved learning all I could about women's health. I guess I became unconsciously selective about what I learned in medical school. My conversations with my friends quickly turned into lessons about the female body. I became a volunteer teacher at the Red Cross, where I would often drift outside of my assigned topic to talk about women's anatomy and women's issues.

My husband would not allow me to go to church, although every year on Christmas we would go to the cathedral and eat communion. However, during my residency training I joined a protestant church and served as the leader for the young women's group. We held very instructive sessions on the female anatomy and birth spacing methods that are completely controlled by the woman. I earned myself a small following and a bigger army of enemies. I received a few unflattering nicknames.

After I graduated from medical school, I was appointed as Deputy Director of the newly created national HIV/AIDS program. I focused my efforts on designing a health education plan for women. We designed a pyramidal flow chart that showed how HIV can spread from one man to about fifty people in as few as five steps. I carried the flow chart in my car and made presentations any time I could: on the side of the street, at the market, in church, etc. My husband had returned home for good after obtaining his PhD in International Relations. He received a high level appointment at the Department of Foreign Affairs. We started to move in diverging directions with our respective careers.

Shortly thereafter my husband's job took us to the west of the country and I was appointed Regional Maternal and Child Health Coordinator. Again, I spent a big part of my time teaching women and offering food and comfort to women in need. I joined the national organization of female physicians and advocated for writing a clinical manual about the practice of female circumcision. Of the half dozen female physicians in the country at that time, only one agreed to do the project with me. We filed the manual in the medical school's library. I don't know if it has ever been used. I also joined the professional women's union and traveled with a group throughout the country to talk to women about basic labor laws and women's rights.

When my troubles with my husband escalated, he arranged to have me demoted. I became just "clinical staff" in a hospital. One day, after I left my husband and went to my mother's house during the weekend, I came to work on Monday to find a note from my boss requesting that I send back the state vehicle. What's more, my whole salary went missing. I showed up at the bank to make a withdrawal from the joint account and they said,

"We did get your automatic salary deposit, but there is no money in this account." Next I was told that I could not access that account any more. I had to completely depend on my husband for all my needs, even though I had a job.

My family had to intercede on my behalf. After my husband came to talk with my family and paid the penalty they requested, they asked me to go back to him. Then, the very next morning when I woke up I discovered that the state car had been returned for me to use. A lot of similar intimidating incidents happened throughout my marriage.

My mother-in-law was very angry with me because I was late giving her a grandchild and, even worse, I never bore her a grandson. She went to my mother's house on two separate occasions to introduce two different young boys and their mothers, and she claimed that my husband was the father of these boys. However, she never personally attacked me. The person who did her dirty job for her was a younger aunt of my husband's. She showed up at my house or office several times with an entourage of women to assault me or pick a fight with me. She even alleged that I was teaching women to rebel against the government, and that they should take my medical license away. I was in a constant struggle mode.

I was not completely isolated – my mother-in-law had six sons and many daughters-in-law. Some of them were not on such good terms with my in-laws either, so they tried to be allies with me. They gave me clues several times that led me to catch my husband cheating on me. They watched over my children so I did not have to hire a babysitter. They helped me in a variety of ways that put them at odds with my mother-in-law and they did not mind it. Some said I had given them the courage to fight back. They said I was their role model.

Many women whose babies I have delivered named the girls after me and showed that they really respected me. Many people in my neighborhood liked me because I helped them with all sorts of ailments and health problems. The women's group that I led in the country continued to function and do good work in the church. To this day, I still receive an occasional phone call from a representative of the group, and this makes me proud. I can only hope that I have helped people in my militancy and zeal to educate more people on the things that I had learned and thought could improve their quality of life.

As for me, there have been people in my life who have helped me in very substantial ways, many of whom I met very briefly and many to whom I never had a chance (or the presence of mind) to say "thank you."

Leaving Home

There was this American woman who was working for USAID's child survival program in my country – my memory is fuzzy as to under which circumstances she befriended me. But I knew that she was very supportive of me, even though she never openly demonstrated it. In our private conversations she always agreed with my positions and sometimes gave me hints or new arguments. I asked her to teach me English. She said the best way to learn English would be for me to visit America and learn it directly through everyday life. So we met secretly to decide on the process, and she endeavored to send applications on my behalf to American institutions for studies of English as a Second Language.

I also had a strong ally at the American embassy, a man from my mother's tribe, who called me his niece. He was a mid-level employee at the consulate department. I believe he did all he could to move my paperwork forward. So I ended up getting something better than I had anticipated: I was accepted into a program of English for Academic Purposes (EAP) which led to an enrollment in a graduate program at a state university in California. A long time passed and I had somehow forgotten about it, consumed as I was with my daily problems. So when my American friend called me to announce that I was accepted into a university in America, I did not know how to react.

I had wished to visit America since the day my high school principal put the idea in my head. I had traveled several times to France. I had been to other countries in Europe like Italy and Germany. I had also visited many countries in Africa: Morocco, Senegal, Mozambique, South Africa, Togo, Benin, Guinea, Ivory Coast, Congo, and Cameroon. The concept of international travel was not new to me. However, this time it was different. This was long-term travel – the first time I would be away from my children for so long.

This happened at a time when I was in a very complicated situation. I had left my husband, but I could not file for divorce, for a variety of reasons. First of all, it was rare for women to initiate a divorce. Rather, it was a man's prerogative to divorce his wife because he had chosen and bought her, and only he had the right to reject her. Secondly, my husband had decided that our marriage was "monogamous". I had caught him with women on several occasions, in my bedroom while my daughters were sleeping in the next room. However, since these were all mistresses, they did not count as worthy to cause a violation of his marriage vow. So in his and my families' judgment, my complaints had no merit and I had absolutely no grounds for leaving the father of my children. I confess that sometimes I questioned my own sanity for continuing to believe that something was wrong while everybody else thought I should feel extremely lucky.

Thirdly, my husband was from a well-to-do family, and he had very wealthy adoptive parents. He had paid in full for my dowry and other material requirements before our marriage. Every time we had an argument and I would go to my mother's home, my relatives would talk to him and ask for money, which he would quickly pay. When that happened, they would gather my stuff while I was in school or at work and delegate two or three men to accompany me. The men would wait for me by the side of the road, preventing me from reentering my mother's house. They would literally take me back to him kicking and screaming or otherwise. And every time I gave birth, they would ask my husband to pay for the "blood". My father's family had this predictable way of asking my husband to give 200,000 *francs* (at the time about 400 dollars) each time I gave birth. When I was pregnant with my second child, my husband knew they were going to ask for money at the time of delivery. So he gave her a middle name that is the phonetic for 200,000 in French. Traditionally, when a man divorces his wife, he can ask for his money back from the in-laws. In my case I knew, and I was clearly told, that my family could never, and would never, repay my husband for all his expenses. Therefore, I should just forget about leaving him. But for some reason, this made me only more determined to get away. I said I would work all my life just to pay him back until the last penny.

Before I left my husband for the last time, I jumped at an opportunity to buy a small parcel next to my mother's home. I then moved to build my own house, just big enough for me and my two daughters. I told myself that nobody could lock me out of my own home or force me to go back to my husband if I was in my own house and on my own land. But when we moved into our new home, my husband came and took the children away. I was not allowed to see them for a whole month. I devised a plan whereby I would go to my firstborn's school after her father dropped her off. I could visit with her during school hours and under the watchful eyes of the teachers. But pretty soon that privilege also was taken away from me. Then I would go and hide in the house of a distant maternal uncle who lived next door to my husband's house. My uncle's children would call on my daughter and ask her to come and play. When she would approach to tell them "no, my father will hit me", I could catch a glimpse of her and I would cry for joy because she was still in one piece and looked very beautiful.

My younger daughter was only two when I left. After a whole month away, I decided I had to go and see her at any cost. I arrived in the middle of the day while my husband was at work. I saw my daughter playing in the yard. She ran to me, then stopped and looked around. I lifted her up and kissed her. She started to shake, literally, for about one minute she was speechless and just shaking. She hugged me as hard as she could and wrapped her arms around my neck. But immediately, my husband's brother came over and started pulling my daughter away from me. He first held her lower side and pulled it away, but her arms were tight around my neck and I held on to her chest as strongly as I could. But he pulled harder and harder on her column, stretching with all his strength; she cried so loudly that the neighbors rushed around. I was very ashamed of the whole scene, but most of all I became really afraid that he was going to break my daughter's vertebrae and hurt her spinal cord. So I quickly kissed my daughter and took her arms off of me. She kept crying and raised her arms toward me as I walked through the crowd and slipped away, very heartbroken. I knew my daughter was thinking that I had forsaken her or betrayed her. She could not understand. Every time I remember that incident I feel a lump in my throat.

Now that I was going to America, the possibility for me to ever see my kids again would vanish forever. But then again, even if I decided to stay, what were the chances that I would get to see them? I was running out of novel and innovative ways to jump over my husband's barriers and hurdles. I decided to go and hoped that God would help me figure the rest out.

The announcement came in May and I had to decide by the end of June, because school was to start in September and I needed enough time to clear all the steps required for the visas. I used a few sleepless nights to think it over, and when I met with my friend a few weeks later, I told her I would go. We kept the details secret. Very few people knew that I was going away for a long time. My family thought I was going to one of the international conferences I regularly attended. I did not speak a word of English, and I did not know enough about America to know what to bring. So I traveled very light. My uncle at the American embassy told me to carry at least fifty dollars on me for incidentals. On the eve of my departure, I went to my uncle's house next to my husband's place, and I stayed there several hours to watch my children play. By now my husband had another woman staying in the house. I did not get to kiss my girls goodbye. I only saw them from afar, through a window. I cried until I grew tired, and I came home.

Once I started English school, I called and told people back home that I was staying for longer than I had told them. It was reported to me that this caused a lot of turmoil. I did not understand the magnitude of the turmoil until much later.

Graduate School
I came to the USA with no English skills whatsoever, so I was given twelve

months to learn the language. By the end of the first semester, I had passed both the Test of English as a Foreign Language (TOEFL) and the Graduate Record Examination (GRE) and I was ready to enter graduate school.

I spent almost all my money in phone bills during that first year. I called home very frequently to speak with my mother and my friends. I told them about the interest that my American classmates showed in learning about our culture. I told them that I had given presentations (despite my very limited English) in a couple of my classes about female circumcision and polygamy. I asked them to please share the information. I told them that I believed the Americans were ahead of the world because they did not bother themselves with keeping secrets. They shared their discoveries and they shared their knowledge very freely. At first, I was intrigued and deriding of such lack of depth or respect for privileged information. But later on, I saw it as a necessary ingredient for long life. All my life I had been keeping secrets after secrets: secrets of the circumcision camp; secrets of my sister's indiscretion; secrets of my husband's abuse; secrets of my mother's annoyance with the Jehovah's Witnesses; secrets of my lack of interest in my marriage; secrets of who helped me against my husband; secrets of sneaking money to my mother; secrets of this, secrets of that. I was full of secrets, and they made me sick and old. That's what I came to believe.

During enrollment in graduate school, I was assigned an academic advisor. But when he met me for the first time and realized I was black and from Africa, he told me he could not work with me; so I was transferred to the only black woman faculty member in the department. She more than welcomed me. She told me that I would do fine if I applied myself. We set up a plan of study, and she explained each step to me slowly and clearly. She asked me what I wanted to learn most of all. I said I was a doctor in my country and I would really appreciate doing something, anything, in a clinical setting while I was going to school. She promised to keep that in mind and she would see what she could do. So at the end of the second semester, when we were ready to do an internship, she made arrangements for me to do mine at La Maestra Family Clinic. She briefed me that the clinic was located in a low-income neighborhood and that I would meet many people there that looked like me. She also said that a mother and daughter team was running the school and clinic, and that in all her time in the city she had never encountered two people more compassionate or more devoted to helping the disadvantaged.

Sure enough, when I was introduced to the clinic, I immediately felt at home. The clinic served mostly immigrant patients from African and Latin American countries. But even more, the staff at the clinic was very diverse:

Mexicans, Filipinos, Salvadorans, Sudanese, Somali, Poles, Ugandans, Kenyans, etc. I had never seen such a mixture of cultures in one small workplace. Our English abilities and our accents varied widely, but we all liked to work with one another. Nobody belittled the others. Instead, after a short while there, you learned to understand English in all its different pronunciations and structures. Just that fact for me was an interesting enough experience to want to show up every chance I got.

This was the first time I experienced the nine-to-six work schedule. I thought it was very long, but the camaraderie there was so appealing that on most days I did not feel it. We met to share a meal every day. One of the nurses regularly organized collections to buy lottery tickets and play for all of us, hoping that one day we'd hit the jackpot and realize our American dream together. There were health fairs and fundraising dinners which were occasions for us to dance, try diverse cuisines and meet the families of other staff members. I started very gradually there, showing up for about ten hours a week. But anytime I stopped at the clinic I was right at home. I could just stay for lunch, or stop by to just go around and say hello; it was always okay. I was always welcome to send a fax or make copies for my school work.

The director and her mother were very helpful, not only in helping me complete my internship assignment, but taking the time to address my personal concerns as well. They helped me find an apartment, took me to the best grocery store, invited me to dinner and gave me gently used clothes. About a year later, when I decided to bring my youngest daughter over, they took the lead in moving the process along. They personally invested in that process, and it was a deciding factor given my limited English abilities and also my ex-husband's position in the Department Of Foreign Affairs back home.

Because of the time difference between the US and my country, I had to make calls late in the night in order to reach people there during business hours. The clinic director's mother willingly spent time with me on the phone in the wee hours of the morning for several days in a row, to make arrangements for my youngest daughter to come join us in the US. She insisted I call from her house, to defray some of the costs. She would sometimes drop short notes on my desk that said, "Remember, you are still a Doctor" or "From one mother to another: everything will be alright". I felt very encouraged by these notes, and I was surprised to see a stranger from a country several times removed actually show me genuine love and appreciation with no criticism, no strings attached.

One of the physicians at the clinic put me in contact with the Educational Commission for Foreign Medical Graduates, where I started the process of trying to get a medical license to practice in the USA. Due to the professional restrictions, I could not function in any clinical capacities. I was limited to my internship in community health, which I completed. I wanted to continue working at the clinic. I was assigned to provide health education and cultural competency consultations to the quickly increasing population of African immigrants.

Through the clinic, I got the opportunity to meet another university faculty member who was working on health issues for women of color. I worked with her on a community survey of women with female circumcision, also called female genital mutilation or female genital cutting by the World Health Organization and the United States. Next, I collaborated with the same professor to write a small grant under the sponsorship of La Maestra Family Clinic. We further expanded the project by holding workshops for public health and nursing students.

I kept my friends and family back home abreast of my activities, and I told them that the United States and the World Health Organization both condemned the practice. I sent documentation to a small group of people I considered to be my allies by fax since email and internet were not readily available in my country. Little did I know that most of these people were never my friends or allies.

After one year, I took a leap of faith and returned home during summer break to see my children. One African man that I had met at the clinic became a mentor to me. He kept in contact with me to advise and support me during my trip. I arrived one afternoon after transfers in New York and Paris. The country was still going through political unrest and a military mutiny against the sitting government. Regular people, however, took advantage of this chaos to settle their personal disputes or exert their own vendettas. Occasionally, stray bullets could cause the death of innocent bystanders, but mostly select people were gunned down in an obscure way, and no one would dare to ask questions.

When my plane landed, we were met at the door by a couple of gentlemen in uniform. They checked our passports and directed us to one of two groups – based on what criteria, I did not know. When we were all sorted out, my small group was told to follow this one guard to a room in the lower level of the airport. We sat there for a while, and then they started calling us in one by one for an interview. When it was my turn I was asked where I was coming from, why I was there, how long I wanted to stay. I said I came to see my children; then I found myself saying, "This is my country. I have a husband here and I will stay as long as he needs me. If he does not need me I can still stay with my mother; she will never kick me out." I wonder why I said that, but immediately my interrogator left and went out to make a phone call. I could hear him saying, "She wants to come back… America is rubbish… What should I do?... Yes Sir…" When he came back he asked me to write the name of my husband down, and sign my name under it. A few minutes later he was joined by a second man who said, "She needs to go to Group C, she needs a lesson… don't trust that..." I started to shake when I heard that.

Shortly after they led me to a small pickup truck and told me to get in the back. There were already a few people in there. I said, "But my luggage is…" They said, "It's going to your husband's house as we speak". They brought in one more person later and then they set us on our way, and told the driver to get going. There were about eight to ten of us travelers and three armed guards in the back of the pickup. Inside the truck were the driver and one other armed person who seemed to be the leader of the group. After we exited the airport and drove for about a mile, they stopped on the shoulder of the road and the leader got out. He went from person to person asking questions, threatening the travelers with beating and torture, and the guards were using their guns to shove the sides of the person being interrogated, and prompting them to "speak up", "answer the Captain" or "shut up".

When it came my turn, the captain looked intently into my eyes and said, "Doctor…?" I said yes. He smiled and shook his head. "Doctor …?" I said, "Yes sir". He paused for a few seconds and said, "Welcome back". He then told the guards "I know everything about her already". So they did not shove me, and he moved to the next person. After they were through we got on our way again. It was very quiet in the truck as we knew we were in trouble. We did not know what we did wrong, where they were taking us, and what was going to happen to each of us. We traveled into the falling night for a while before the truck stopped in a somber side of town that I had difficulties making out. The leader got out, the three guards jumped down and he gave them some directions, then said goodbye. Before he left, he called me up and asked me to hand my purse over. I obliged. It contained only a few documents and a twenty dollar bill. At this point, I was more worried about my life than about a purse. He took the purse and asked one of the guards to help me get down. They held my hands and I jumped onto the concrete road. He said, "Put your shoes on," and I did. He said "move" but I kept my eyes on him because I had been told they would never shoot you if you were looking straight at them. They would wait for you to turn your back before they shoot you. So I started stepping backward in the dark, slowly. He said a few more words to them and turned to meet me as the truck sped away. He had put his gun in the pocket on his side, and was carrying my purse on one hand, and a big duffle bag on the other hand. I said a quick prayer and asked God to protect my daughters and allow my mother to die in dignity. I had not even told my mother I was coming home. I knew that the moment she heard about my death she would pass out, so I prayed that she would not suffer too much but instead join me quickly in heaven.

After a few steps and while I was still saying my prayer, the man put down everything and just grabbed me in a big hug. I was flabbergasted. I had never met this guy before, I thought to myself. Who was he? He said, :Doctor …, I am so glad I found you today. I always thought I would never repay you for literally saving my father's and my daughter's lives. Today I saved your life. Now I am glad we are even." He laughed out loud and said again, "We are even; I paid my debt, God!"

I followed him for a short walk, deep into the area to his home, where I met his father, whose face I did recognize. The old man had a strangulated hernia one holiday morning when I was on call, and I had operated on him, then I came out and announced to his accompanying son (now the leader of the rebels) that he would be fine. They reported that I showed up the next day with breakfast from the student's lounge and gave it to the patient, who shared with his son. They were thankful. That same young man was the father of a toddler who became gravely ill and they rushed her to the hospital one evening while I was rotating in Pediatrics. The young father heard me say that I suspected the little girl had meningitis. It was time for me to go home and I was telling a classmate that my husband would definitely kill me for being late, but I'd take care of this young girl and take the beating rather than leave and bear the guilt of letting her die. He remembered that I had to run to another part of the hospital on two separate occasions to get equipment and material for the spinal tap and for IV fluid administration. He said I took very good care of the girl, and she survived only because I did what I did. He said when he saw me in the pediatric ward taking care of his baby, he knew she was in good hands. He was watching through the windows while the baby's mother was with me in the room.

That night I was welcomed like a long lost family member; they gave me food, but I was too shaken up to eat. He warned me to be very, very careful. However, he said, no member of his gang would hurt me. He gave me a card to present if ever I fell again into the hands of rebels. I was too afraid to ask why they had detained me and what would have happened had he not recognized me. He did not tell me either.

I asked him to call my best friend Vickie, who sent her husband on a motorcycle to pick me up and take me to mother's house under the cover of night. My mother and I were very happy just because I was home safe and sound. I never asked for my luggage. As soon as I could, I made it to the American embassy to request a dependent visa for my firstborn. I thought I could not bring two kids with me to America and still be able to go to school fulltime, as I should. Also, I doubted that my husband would let both kids get out of his sight without suspicion. The gang leader came to the embassy to testify in my favor. What he said confidentially to them there scared everyone: the consul general, my uncle who worked at the embassy, even the secretary. All thought that I had cheated death. I told them I did not want to know the details. I was too afraid already. I gave a brief account of the ordeal to my mentor back in San Diego via fax. He grew very concerned as well. He asked me to come back as quickly as I could.

With help from people in my mother-in-law's household, a relative asked my husband permission to take the girl out for a visit to her grandma, when in reality they were meeting me at the airport. A half hour later we were on the plane to South Africa (no more going through Paris, it was too risky), and back to the USA. When my friend and mentor picked us up at the San Diego airport, he was frozen with emotion. It probably brought to his memory some of the tragedies in his own Uganda, and the kind of hurdles some mothers go through for their offspring. Before I left, I introduced a divorce request with the court, and named my sister to act as my surrogate. My husband did not contest.

Three years later, when I surmised that my ex-husband's anger had started to subside and that he may be amenable to letting his guard down, I sent for my youngest child. A few friends in the neighborhood helped with getting her picture for the passport. The director of the San Diego clinic along with her mother and sister helped me with the visa application and the ticket. Given the prohibitive cost of the ticket (over $2000) I could never have engaged in this mission without their help. My niece was in charge of informing my daughter about how the process was coming along. Thankfully, everyone knew how to keep a secret. It came in handy.

The airplane was slated to depart at 6:00 pm. My daughter had cooked that day for her father and when he came back from work she served him; he ate and decided he would take a nap. That's when my niece showed up for a visit. Shortly after, my daughter got up to walk her cousin out as she was leaving. Instead, the two turned a corner and got into a taxi that took them to a friend's house. Fortunately, that friend was a lawyer. He was careful to register my daughter as a "private guest from the prosecutor" on the airport list. When my daughter arrived, he phoned the airline to inquire whether the plane would be on time. He was told the plane was late out of Brazzaville and would depart at 11:00 pm instead. So he hid her in one of his kids' rooms.

When my ex-husband woke up and found out the girl had gone, he rushed to my mother's house and looked everywhere. He badmouthed them, and went straight to the airport. There he was told that everyone who showed up for the trip was still there, because they just had gotten the news that the plane would be late. Of course he looked and saw no sign of my daughter or anyone from my family, so he went home and focused his search locally. I believe he underestimated how many people were on my side, not because I deserved it, but in part because he had gone too far.

Meanwhile, I was a real nervous wreck. I could not sleep. I had no way of checking on my baby once she left. All I could do was pray and hope. I had to avoid calling my mother because I knew my ex-husband would be there or know of it. Two whole days and five plane changes later, my daughter landed in Los Angeles and I was there to hug her, for the first time since that day when her uncle snatched her out of my embrace seven years back.

Today
My daughters are now fully integrated in the American society; they have become independent young women with career goals to pursue and jobs to attend to. They are helping their father financially whenever they can. He recently visited the US to participate in the marriage of my younger daughter; he insisted that the groom pay a dowry in keeping with our African tradition. My son-in-law agreed and gave him the requested amount in cash. He never felt the need to discuss any of this with me, and it is just fine by me.

Besides my two kids, I was also able to sponsor my older brother along with his family. Thanks to his coming to America, he has cleaned up his life and now has a loving relationship with his wife and seven children here in California. He himself is surprised at this 180 degree change that occurred in his life. My mother has made the trip as well. At eighty years old, she has long passed the life expectancy of about forty-six years for women in my country. She is still strong and enjoying her great-grandchildren. Her first great-grandchild is now seventeen years old and I am praying that she live long enough to see a great-great-grandchild.

As for me, I am forever grateful for the turn my life has taken. I am settled in America with clear goals to pursue and unlimited possibilities. I have freedom to live my life and make informed decisions about my life without any fear of beatings, unlawful retribution or unwarranted oppression. Last year, I had just moved to take a job in the Midwest and was experiencing the harsh winter they are so used to. One day full of ice and snow, I tried to run across the street and suddenly found myself on the ground. I did not realize immediately that I had fallen. After all that was the first time I had fallen in about eighteen years! A Good Samaritan noticed that I must be a newcomer, so he rushed over to help me up. For a moment there, when I lifted up my eyes and saw this man over me with his hand stretched out, my mind went back to when my husband would knock me down me while he whipped me. So I screamed hard and started sliding and rolling on the ice. Two more people joined the man as they pulled me up and planted me on my feet. They asked if I was okay. They wanted to help me to my car. I mumbled something in utter embarrassment. They could not understand it. They had not the slightest idea. I cancelled every appointment I had that day and went straight home. I took the day to work on myself and keep on getting this old idea out of my head. I was now in America, a land of law and respect. I needed to put that in my head. I still need to learn that.

QUESTIONS

1. Where did Fabienne grow up?

2. What was her family structure like?

3. Were girls conditioned the same as boys were in the family structure? Did they have the same goals set for their futures? Was this evident at an early age?

4. Was education easily accessible for all children?

5. What kind of student was Fabienne?

6. How did Fabienne's family react to her thirst for education? Was she encouraged to become educated? Do you think Fabienne had to suppress her desire to pursue education?

7. What did Fabienne play with as a child?

8. What values did Fabienne's mother teach her?

9. What religion did Fabienne's family practice? How did the villagers react toward people who did not practice the same religion?

10. How was Fabienne treated by her brother?

11. Was Fabienne ostracized for being different from her peers?

12. How did Fabienne's family welcome strangers?

13. What work did Fabienne's father do?

14. What was Fabienne's mother expected to do when her husband died?

15. How did Fabienne's family obtain the funds necessary to support the household? How did Fabienne begin to help with her family's expenses?

16. Why did Fabienne decide to become a doctor? Was her mother supportive of her decision to become a doctor?

17. Why did Fabienne's siblings call her "Miss Education"?

18. How did Fabienne's mother's advice about not being "prideful" affect Fabienne?

19. Did Fabienne's husband encourage her educational pursuits?

20. What forms of abuse did Fabienne suffer at the hand of her husband? How did she deal with this abuse? Do you think that she had any other option than to react as she did?

21. What form of government existed in the Central African Republic during Fabienne's childhood?

22. What did the president do each time his wife gave birth?

23. When did the president crown himself Emperor?

24. What national holiday did he institute?

25. What challenges did Fabienne face in her pursuit of a career as a doctor?

26. What role did Fabienne's high school principal play in her education?

27. According to Fabienne's mother-in-law, why was Fabienne's first child born a girl instead of a boy?

28. How did Fabienne get into medical school? What was her husband's reaction?

29. What challenges did Fabienne face during medical school?

30. How did Fabienne's marriage affect her relationship with her mother?

31. How did Fabienne help to support her mother?

32. Where did Fabienne do her residency training? What did she pick for her thesis?

33. What was the proudest moment of Fabienne's life?

34. Who advised Fabienne to go to the US?

35. In Fabienne's culture, what traditional ceremony marked the passage of childhood to womanhood? Where was this ceremony carried out?

Why did girls look forward to this ceremony?   How did Fabienne prepare for it?

36. How did the girls feel on the way to the camp?   How did this change?

37. What role did the chaperone play in the camp?

38. How long was Fabienne in the camp?

39. Who performed the procedure?

40. How were the girls punished in the camp, and for what?

41. What skills did the girls learn at the camp?

42. What happened to Marianne?   How did Fabienne feel about what happened?

43. What happened to some of the other girls who came back from the camp?

44. What are some of the lasting effects that resulted from Fabienne's circumcision?

45. How did Fabienne first become aware of who her future husband would be?

46. What was Fabienne's role in her future husband's family?

47. What did Fabienne's future mother-in-law regularly have her checked for?

48. Why was it a dilemma for Fabienne when her menstruation began?

49. How did Fabienne feel about her body?

50. What did Fabienne think about her husband to be, when she finally met him?   Was her husband happy with this arranged marriage?

51. How many wives were men allowed to have in Fabienne's culture?   At the civil wedding, why did Fabienne's husband declare that he would have only one wife?

52. How was Fabienne's life different after marriage?

53. Why did Fabienne nurse a child that wasn't hers? How was she able to accomplish this? What was Fabienne's husband's reaction when he found her nursing this child?

54. How old was Fabienne when she had her first child?

55. Why did Fabienne join student marches?

56. When did Fabienne begin to learn about the circumcision procedure from a medical viewpoint?

57. What happened to Fabienne when she joined the protestant church?

58. Where did Fabienne volunteer as a teacher? What did she teach?

59. What position did Fabienne take after graduating from medical school?

60. What topic and program did she focus on? What were some of her outreach activities?

61. What position did Fabienne's husband obtain? When they moved, what job did Fabienne take?

62. How did Fabienne get demoted?

63. How did Fabienne's husband obtain control of her salary?

64. How did Fabienne's family intercede for her with her husband? Why did she return to him?

65. How did Fabienne's mother-in-law treat her? What was Fabienne's relationship with her sisters-in law like?

66. How did Fabienne arrange to come to the US?

67. Why didn't Fabienne file for divorce when she left her husband? How did her family benefit from her continuing the marriage?

68. How did Fabienne manage to purchase a piece of land?

69. What was Fabienne's husband's reaction to Fabienne moving into her own house? What did he do?

70. Did Fabienne think she would be able to see her daughters again

when she left for the US?

71. Did Fabienne's husband and family know she was planning to go to the US?

72. What was Fabienne's life like during her first year in the US?

73. What information did Fabienne share with her family when she called them? What secrets did she keep from them?

74. Where did Fabienne intern during graduate school in the US? How did she feel at the internship site? What were some of her observations about the site?

75. How did Fabienne come to take part in providing workshops for public health and nursing students?

76. What did Fabienne do to promote the condemnation of female genital mutilation in her country of origin while living in the US?

77. When did Fabienne return to the Central African Republic for a visit?

78. What happened upon her arrival? Who rescued her from this experience? What do you think would have happened if she had not been recognized?

79. Where did Fabienne seek refuge after her ordeal?

80. When did Fabienne file for divorce?

81. How many years had passed since Fabienne held her second daughter? How was she able to bring her to the US? What challenges did she overcome to do this?

82. What was her husband's reaction?

83. How did Fabienne feel during this ordeal?

84. How did Fabienne's coming to the US help further the cause to prevent FGM?

85. How did Fabienne's daughters fare in the US? What kind of future would her daughters have had if they had stayed with their father?

86. What kind of relationship exists now between Fabienne's daughters and their father?

87. In what ways is Fabienne "free" now in the US? What has she achieved here?

88. What value has Fabienne brought to her new country?

89. What personal characteristics have helped Fabienne survive so many years of suffering?

90. Is Fabienne a "survivor" or a "thriver" now?

John Kueck's Story

Akobo

John Kueck was born in 1970 in Akobo, Southern Sudan. Akobo is a large district, but not large enough to be qualified as a city. John's family lived in a village of approximately 5000-6000 people, one of five villages that surrounded the town of Akobo. The closest city, Malakal, was a two to three day drive away from his village and Juba, the capital of Southern Sudan and the largest city, was about a four to five day drive. Although the distances between John's village and the closest cities were not great, the poor road conditions made car travel especially time-consuming.

John lived in a *tukul*, a round structure made of wood and mud with a pointed grass roof. The tukul had another hut on the side for the family's animals. Children lived with their mother in the main tukul. In John's village, if the family was wealthy, the father would live in a third tukul on the side opposite the animals' hut and if he had a second wife and more children, they would live there also. The door of the main tukul was three feet tall, hinged at the top, and inhabitants were forced to bend down to enter and leave the house. The door was thick, made of tightly wound grass, vines and wood. A string attached to a heavy piece of wood would secure the door. Some villagers hung aluminum sheets on the outside of their doors to attach locks. In contrast, the houses in the town of Akobo were constructed of adobe bricks with full-size doors and aluminum sheet roofs, with a shape similar to houses in the United States.

Each morning, as John crouched through the opening of the family tukul, the first thing he would see were the cows. His father would have already released the livestock to feed and exercise them. John's family owned twenty cows, along with some sheep and a few goats. Behind the house was a three-acre farm where the family's main crop was sorghum grain, in addition to a variety of beans, pumpkins, peanuts, sesame and corn. A common dish was whole corn cooked with beans, butter and salt. In front of John's house were trees and long grass. Southern Sudan was full of trees, including lots of tamarind. Some trees bore sweet yellow date-shaped fruit and others a brown and green fruit similar to seeded grapes. The summer season ran from June to August, and John recalls the familiar scent of flowers and soil. Summer was followed by the dusty and windy months of autumn, and during the winter months, October to December, the air always smelled of water. John worked contentedly alongside his father, tending to the livestock and the farm.

John was the oldest surviving child in his family. Although his mother had another before him, that child had died at age two. When John was born, his mother named him Chuol, meaning repayment - payment for the child which had been lost. Since John was the oldest, and also the only male child, he enjoyed particular favoritism. His parents refused to allow him to be punished. If he was reprimanded by one parent, he would run to the other for refuge. Even his younger sisters were forbidden to harass him, as he was the future leader of the family. John identifies with Simba, the young lion from *The Lion King* movie. He knew from an early age that he would ascend to the throne, and he was given all due deference.

When John was just seven years old, his mother died giving birth to his youngest sister. His mother had not been well during the pregnancy, and had lost a significant amount of blood. The nearest hospital was a three-day journey by foot and, although his mother made it there, she did not return. Following her death, John's aunt and uncle invited him to come live with them in Akobo so that he could attend school. The acceptance rate for school was extremely low, with families relying on their political connections or paying excessive sums of money. John's uncle had military connections and he called on them to help John secure a place at the school, which was located on the border with Ethiopia. John attended the school for three months before his father came to take him back home. As the only other man in the family, John's father needed him to help tend to the farm and animals. John's aunt knew what was best for John, and she did not give up so easily. She waited for an opportune time to approach John's father again, pleading with him on behalf of the boy's education. His father eventually relented, and John returned to the school dormitory. It was here that he learned to speak Amharic. Three months later, John's father retrieved him once more, and they both returned to the family farm. John was fourteen years old, with almost no education.

After his mother's death, John's father had been reluctant to remarry. He was concerned about how a new wife might treat his children. Five years later, John's father finally arranged to marry. But when the bride's family demanded an excessive dowry, he called the whole thing off. He was unwilling to squander his family's assets on a dowry. When John was almost fifteen, his aunt came to live with them in the village. Her husband had divorced her because she was barren and, in their culture, that was perfectly acceptable grounds for divorce. His aunt helped John's father take care of the younger children, a great relief in their mother's absence.

Not long after, John's father became gravely ill. The symptoms began like the flu, but he never recuperated from them. He spent the next six months in bed. John's uncle took him to see a doctor in Akobo, but it did not help. The family collected money to transport John's father to the city of Khartoum, but he died before he could make the trip. The cause of death was not determined, since there were no autopsies. This left John as head of the household, with sole responsibility for the family, the livestock and farm. John's uncle on his father's side had begun stealing the cows, sheep and goats while John's father lie in bed dying. John felt helpless because he was still young and technically not yet a man. It was only when John turned fifteen later that year that he could lawfully defend his family's property. This was a very difficult period for John, who, betrayed by his uncle, did not have the legal authority to challenge him.

Manhood
According to Nuer tradition, upon turning fifteen, all males participate in a ceremony to mark their arrival into manhood. Typically fifteen to thirty boys would participate at one time. It was up to the boys to find a "specialist" to travel to the village to perform the markings and the initiation ceremony. The boys' families would agree on a date for the ceremony, and a fee to be paid to the specialist. It was an elaborate ceremony, taking place over several days. Relatives would come from far and wide to participate in the momentous occasion. The first phase involved the marking of their foreheads. Next, the boys would enter a house, where they would stay for the duration of their initiation, until they graduated fifteen to twenty days later. During this time, they received special treatment: food was prepared for them, and while they sat around, eating and visiting, they would enjoy an occasional visit from a tribal elder, speaking with them about the responsibilities of manhood. Responsibilities included the right to defend one's property, the right to have girlfriends, and the right to marry. The boys were allowed outside of the initiation house only late in the evening when they could avoid being seen by other villagers.

Festivities began after the boys graduated from the initiation phase. There was a huge celebration. Heads were shaved, and hats were provided to cover their foreheads during the day, but could be removed in the evenings. Upon graduating, fathers presented their sons with special tokens in recognition of their arrival into manhood. Spears and guns were customary, as they symbolized bravery. More information about the Nuer ceremony can be found in the book *The Nuer: A Description of the Modes of Livelihood and Political Institutions of a Nilotic People*, by E. E. Evans-

Pritchard.

Akobo Tribes

Most of the people in the village John grew up in were members of the tribe called Nuer. Other tribes are Dinka, Chiluk (*pronounced "Shiluk"*), Anuak and Murle (*pronounced "Murlay"*). The district of Akobo is considered a Nuer province, since the majority of the inhabitants are of that tribe. The villages surrounding Akobo quarreled with each other constantly. It was common practice for the Anuak and Murle tribes to rustle cattle from the neighboring Nuer village, which prompted considerable conflict in the reclaiming. The Sudanese government did what it could to maintain some measure of peace; otherwise, the fighting would have been much worse.

Members of the Nuer tribe are held in high regard for their bravery and their accomplishments. Their roots are steeped in tradition, and they are the only tribe to have owned private land. The Nuer are self-reliant, tending to large farms and livestock, while remaining within the province to work. It is said that the Nuer people originated in Bentio in the upper Nile region of Egypt. They then migrated towards Ethiopia, on the border with Sudan, to the Anuak tribal lands. As the Nuer migrated south, they carried with them the language and architectural elements of the Bentio culture. Throughout history, the Nuer would battle neighboring tribes, capturing rival members to add to their own village. It is not surprising then that the Nuer tribe was a blend of Dinka, Anuak, Murle and also Chai (*pronounced "Shai"*), who came from the border with Ethiopia.

To differentiate themselves from other tribes, rival members display distinct body markings – most commonly across their foreheads. The mark for the Nuer men consists of six horizontal lines across the forehead. If two brothers are marked on the same day, the elder will get seven lines instead of six, but instances of this kind are rare. The Dinka tribe marks both their men and their women with horizontal and vertical lines. The Chiluk display a single line across the forehead, composed of large sequential dots. Similar to the Chiluk's is the Anuak tribal mark, but the dots are very small. Members of the Murle tribe do not display traditional forehead marks, but instead remove the lower front four teeth. This is typically done somewhere between the age of three and five, with both genders participating. It is considered a sign of beauty to have a small mouth. It is believed that by removing these teeth the mouth will be small. Women of all tribes display random dot markings on their faces, also considered signs of beauty.

Each tribe's language is different and, although all tribes raise cows and utilize nearly the same basic cooking ingredients, there are differences in each one's dishes and in the variety of spices they favored.

Worship & Superstition

As recently as three generations ago, the people of the Akobo tribes had, with rare exception, converted to either Islam or to Christianity. There were some who still chose to worship other gods, but they were relatively few.

Before then, the Nuer worshipped a God called Ngundeng (*pronounced "Moondang"*), which translates to "gift from a higher god." The premise for the religion is the story of an old woman and her husband who were barren. One day God spoke to them, telling the couple that He would be sending them a child. Just as God had said, the woman, eighty years old at the time, gave birth to a son. The old couple named their son Ngundeng. It was believed that Ngundeng had been sent by God to save his people. He became a prophet and performed miracles for all to see. He asked his people to construct a pyramid surrounded by elephant tusks and they did. Ngundeng told the people that after his death, they were to look at the new moon on the third day to see him waving over the moon. The people of Southern Sudan believed that their power to survive came from Ngundeng's protection.

When John was a child, he remembers watching a group of people assembled in a large circle, in an area about the size of a football stadium, singing and chanting while cows were slaughtered in sacrifice to their God. They tossed water and wine and rich foods high into the air as an offering. Other tribes had different devotions, and some worshipped stone gods who spoke to them. Many of the village homes had symbols displayed at the entrance, like small trees guarding the premises. These days though, most of the people of Southern Sudan have long since abandoned their worship of other gods. Information about the religions of Southern Sudan can be found in the book *Nuer Prophets: A History of Prophecy from the Upper Nile in the Nineteenth and Twentieth Centuries*, by Douglas H. Johnson.

Every tribe has superstitions. They believe that curses can kill, and they believe in the evil eye. Members of the Sudanese community in San Diego believe that American Indian tribes have magic, and to associate with them will bring them good luck and possibly even magical powers. It is believed that at least one Native American tribe shares the Nuer's reverence for their god, Ngundeng, as well as performance of their same rituals.

Hierarchy

There are three classes in all tribal structures. Elders garner the most respect; young men in the tribe come second, and last are the women. Decisions for the tribe are made by the elders: they intercede to resolve conflict and are consulted in arrangements of marriages and dowries. The elders are the ones responsible for carrying on the traditions of the tribe, and insuring that the tribal dynamics remain intact.

War

The war in Southern Sudan, a revolt against the Khartoum military government, began when John was quite young. Rebels organized into one group in Juba, headed by the Equatorian tribe, and that organization evolved into a second, run primarily by the Nuer tribe. Later still, a third organization emerged, led predominantly by the Dinka tribe. This group was called the SPLA, *Sudanese People's Liberation Army*. The SPLA took control of the Ethiopian border, as their strongest assistance came from the Ethiopian government. They began to fight against the Nuer group, but later made peace and joined forces to become the strongest rebel force in Southern Sudan. The Dinka tribe continued to dominate the SPLA.

John was fifteen when people in his village started to disappear. The Khartoum military would raid the villages surrounding Akobo in an effort to root out rebel fighters hiding within their boundaries. They rounded up groups of men randomly, killing them or taking them to distant towns. Their strategy was to relocate or kill enough village men until the rebellion was finally weakened. John and his family were among those displaced. They traveled to the border of Ethiopia, to a large refugee camp with a population of approximately 30,000, called Itang. While in the camp, John found a distant relative, whom he referred to as "Uncle John." John had met him years earlier when he visited the family's village to immunize the cows. Uncle John (John Kang) worked as the Itang camp veterinarian, though he often helped provide medical services for the refugees as well.

Itang Refugee Camp

John and his family lived in the camp, located on the East/West border between Sudan and Ethiopia, for four years. Life at the camp was extremely grueling. Although the United Nations provided food, it was insufficient, and there was no potable water to be had. Refugees were forced to drink the dirty, contaminated river water. Thousands died from cholera, typhoid, tuberculosis and malaria. Scabies was also very common. There was a single doctor in a single health clinic to serve all 30,000 refugees. The sick would line up the night before in hopes of getting medical attention. The doctor and all three nurses were Ethiopian, so there was a language barrier as well. At 6:00 am, one nurse would walk along the line of people, kicking the ill and recording their symptoms in an attempt to prioritize those with the most serious conditions. After the somewhat brutal triage procedure, just twenty cards would be issued. Only those who received a card would see the doctor that day, and the rest would camp overnight again and again, until their turn to be one of the twenty.

Once the doctor was finished examining the patient, he or she would be sent to the adjoining tent for any medicine that had been prescribed. In most cases the medicine was provided on the same day, but sometimes the pharmacy ran dry. The refugees placed very little faith in the medical care, as the results were seldom positive. Many patients died in spite of the care, and the general sentiment was that a trip to the doctor was a waste of time. Refugees blamed the Ethiopian government for the lack of doctors and in 1986 Sudanese nurses were brought in to assist the Ethiopian doctor. This helped with the language and cultural barriers. The Itang camp was a joint venture between the Ethiopian government and the SPLA. The refugees felt that the treatment from the guards, although severe, was more humane due to their SPLA representation.

It was in Itang that John was finally able to continue his studies, as the United Nations provided education in the camp. In 1986, he completed his seventh grade basic education. He continued with his studies for another eighteen months to earn what is equivalent to an LVN or medical assistant certification. When the SPLA announced examinations for a handful of vocational training slots, John was one of the two-hundred fifteen refugees who passed the exam. Following three months of training, John was accepted into the eighteen-month certification course required to become a registered nurse. The teachers were all Ethiopian, and they would expel students randomly without apparent reason. The students took great care to humor the teachers to avoid being expelled from the course. Of the initial two-hundred fifteen students, only a quarter graduated. John felt blessed to be one of the fortunate few.

There were three therapeutic tents, about three hundred square feet each, which housed the patients with the most serious conditions. One of John's duties was to make night checks on those who were critically ill. He made the rounds without aid of electricity, and the single gas lantern suspended from the ceiling of each tent did little to improve the otherwise stark darkness. In the morning, it was John's responsibility to count the number of patients who had failed to survive the night. John served as a nurse at Itang camp until the year 1990, when the Ethiopian ruler, Mengistu Haile Mariam, was relieved of power. When his successor, Meles Zenawi, came to power, all of the refugees were expelled from camp. In fear for their survival, the again displaced refugees returned to Southern Sudan. The United Nations followed the former emigrants' migration toward home, handing out tents and food to John and his fellow villagers. Upon their return, the refugees found only disappointment. The farms had not been tended, and the crops were all dead.

Return to Akobo

As soon as the family had returned to Akobo, John's aunt began pressing him to take a wife. She pointed out to him the advantageous timing, as they still had cows for a dowry. John did not agree with his aunt, as he longed to return to Ethiopia to continue his studies. He could not see the point in getting married only to leave a bride behind. Around that time, a friend of John's returned from Ethiopia to escape the killings that had become commonplace there. Anuak police were targeting Nuer tribal members who had been expelled from the refugee camp. John realized that it was not a prudent time to be traveling in Ethiopia. John's aunt continued to press the marriage topic. She promised John that he could continue his studies, and that his bride could stay in her home during John's courses at school. John began to give in, understanding that if he waited too long they might not have cows left for the dowry. John knew of a girl named Rebecca, another member of the Nuer tribe who he had met while studying in Ethiopia. They had become acquainted at the Presbyterian Church where they both sang in the choir. John didn't know her current whereabouts, but he did know her parents' names and the village where she had come from. His aunt and uncle began making inquiries immediately about the girl and her family. It turned out that there had been a marriage between the two families before. So, satisfied with the details they had learned about the girl and her family, they gave John their blessing.

John and his uncle set out on foot to travel to the town of Nasir, a full day's journey away. They inquired at the church on the morning after their arrival, and learned that Rebecca lived in a village across the river. That was another day's journey by foot. Upon inquiring at the church in the village where she lived, they learned that Rebecca's house was the one next door. Rebecca's mother served as deacon of the church. Church members were sent to bring Rebecca to meet John and his uncle. When Rebecca entered the church, she was both surprised and delighted to see John. She hadn't known what had happened to him since they became separated in Ethiopia, and the two talked and caught up for the next two hours. John and his uncle arranged a time for the couple to meet with Rebecca's family.

During the meeting, John discussed his intentions and his offering for the dowry. He and his uncle explained John's intent to bring Rebecca to live with his family, while he continued his studies in Ethiopia. The thought of leaving her family was a difficult one for Rebecca. However, she and her family discussed it, agreed that the terms for the marriage were acceptable and set a wedding date for the following December. The wedding took place in Nasir, which was the half-way point between Akobo and Ulang, the village where Rebecca and her family lived. The cows would be given at the wedding. The remaining livestock would be delivered in January, after the rainy season.

John and Rebecca exchanged vows during two ceremonies. The first was held in the church, as both families were of the Christian faith. On the following day, a traditional ceremony was held. Both families began dancing early in the morning, and by 1:00 pm, guests begin arriving to join in the dance, to eat and to drink. On the third day, John took his bride to his home in Akobo.

There was no work or promise of work in Southern Sudan so, in 1993, John left his new bride, already pregnant with their first daughter, in search of work in Ethiopia. John had heard that the government at that time was allowing students with lower-level certifications to further their studies. John found work in the Fugnido refugee camp.

Fugnido Refugee Camp
The Fugnido camp was located on the Southern border between Sudan and Ethiopia, in the area where the Anuak tribe lived. There were 15,000 to 20,000 refugees in Fugnido when John arrived, once again supported by the United Nations. Various church organizations operated in the camp, conducting daily prayers. The United Nations ran a school for children through the seventh grade.

The United Nations contracted with the Ethiopian government to provide health care for the camp's refugees. John worked as a nurse, alongside two Ethiopian nurses, assisting the one Ethiopian doctor. They U.N. officials were shown lists with a general accounting of refugees, but lacked accurate statistics as to how many had perished, and from what causes. The camp lacked a laboratory to correctly diagnose the illnesses. Medications provided by the U.N. were distributed via the Ethiopian government and few reached the intended destination. As a result, many who would have survived died due to the lack of medicine. During John's time in the camp clinic, he witnessed firsthand the underreporting of deaths. He was also privy to the siphoning off of medications. In addition, the U.N. provided blankets, food and eating utensils but again only a small portion of what was sent reached the refugees.

The reports to the U.N. were prepared by the Sudanese, who were located in the camp headquarters. The reports went from there to the Ethiopian government, where they were amended before reaching the U.N. officials. When officials from the United Nations came to inspect the camp, they were shown specific tents, spoke only with predetermined people, and sampled water from a fountain, declaring it clean. They were completely unaware that the camp had only two drinking fountains, and that the refugees drank from the river.

The tents were small – only about five feet by ten for an entire family.

The size of the family did not matter; only one tent per family was issued. It was not uncommon for ten people to share a tent. Inside the tents, it was cold at night and hot during the day. When the wind blew, the dust permeated everything. Rain caused mud, and the mud seeped into the tents. There were dirt paths, but no paved roads.

The Fugnido Camp was run by the Ethiopian government. The guards were Ethiopian and they made every effort to insure that the refugees felt less than human. They were abusive, and would routinely pick someone at random to verbally and physically abuse. In most cases, the bullying was without provocation. Sometimes the guards would select an ill person waiting outside the clinic as the victim for their abuse. They would kick and beat them or curse at them, or sometimes chase them out of line. Some believed that they did this as a way to cut down on the number of people seeking access to healthcare.

The police were hired from the Anuak tribe, who were longtime enemies of the Nuer tribe. Therefore, the Nuer refugees had no say in the operations at the camp, nor in the treatment they received. They were at the sole mercy of the Ethiopian guards and the Anuak policemen. Rape was a common occurrence, as were random beatings and killings.

There were no jobs to be had, and since the refugees were not allowed to farm the land, they sat idle. In addition to food, clothing and other necessities, Ethiopian traders sold alcohol, which was a major contributor to camp crime. To earn money to purchase the traders' goods, refugees would gather wood from the forests to sell in the villages. Others would hoard their rations, knowing they could sell it to others when food came up short – usually once every two weeks.

John earned 150 *birr*, equivalent to 30 US dollars, for his work as a camp nurse. He sent a letter along with someone traveling to Akobo, requesting that his wife and daughter join him at the camp. Rebecca arrived a month later, along with their newborn daughter. John and his family remained in the camp for two years, while John saved as much money as he could.

John learned that from nearby Kenya, he and his family would be able to apply for resettlement in Canada or the United States. He paid a smuggler to sneak him and his family across the border. Unfortunately, their attempt failed and they were arrested and sentenced to thirty days in prison. At month's end, they were released, robbed of their possessions and deported back to the Ethiopian side of the border. John and his family were left with nothing. A Nuer tribesman, known as the "Ambassador", learned of John's situation. Married to a Kenyan woman, the Ambassador was able to cross over the border to bring them food and money to pay for a hotel room. He continued to provide support to the family for the next three months. The hotel owner took pity on the family's circumstances, discounting the room rate and occasionally bringing them food.

The Ambassador was able to secure travel documents for John and his family, and paid to have them pass safely across the border. Although they would have preferred to go to Nairobi, it was quite expensive and jobs were scarce. Instead, John and his family were directed to another refugee camp called IFO, located in eastern Kenya, along the border with Somalia.

IFO Refugee Camp
IFO Camp contained 5,000 Sudanese and 100,000 Somali and Somali Bantu refugees. The Bantu tribe originated in Tanzania and were brought by slave traders to Somalia from the Indian Ocean coast. After human rights laws abolished slavery, the Bantu remained in Somalia, retaining their native language and customs. The Bantu did not integrate well with the Somali. In the camp, fights broke out between them, so the Bantu were assigned a separate area within the camp. John attempted to find work, but since there were so few jobs available in Nairobi, there was already an abundance of Kenyan doctors and nurses working in the camp.

John and his family lived in the camp for two years before they could start the resettlement process, which included a heap of applications and medical examinations. The United States INS covered the cost for the examinations. Refugees who tested positive for HIV or Hepatitis B were not allowed to immigrate into the US, as those were considered communicable diseases. At the time, approximately two percent of the Sudanese population in the camp tested positive for HIV. Some tested positive for syphilis and had their infections treated. Others were told they had "bad syphilis" and were also denied resettlement. Those who failed the medical tests were left in the camp to die. The resettlement process took John and his family three months.

An organization called the International Rescue Committee focused their efforts on helping the Lost Boys of Sudan. These were boys who had been displaced or orphaned during the Second Sudanese Civil War. Many were taken from their family villages to be conscripted into the army when they were just ten to fifteen years old. By the time they entered the Itang camp, they were already considered soldiers. When the Lost Boys were relocated to the Fugnido camp, the SPLA chose not to integrate them with the general camp population, but instead provided them with a separate area in camp to live and continue formal military training. When Ethiopia changed leadership and the camps closed, the Lost Boys were sent to Southern Sudan along the Kenyan border where the Murle and Anuak tribes lived. Although most of the boys were from the Nuer and Dinka tribes, they were not returned home to their families. The boys, numbering approximately two hundred fifty, were protected by the SPLA soldiers until the border opened and they were allowed to cross into Kenya. These two hundred fifty boys were insignificant in number when compared to the hundreds of thousands of Sudanese refugees, but because of the support of the International Rescue Committee, the Lost Boys were granted special consideration. Sadly, without a traditional family upbringing, the Lost Boys were as ill-prepared to fit in with the refugee community and later in mainstream America.

United States
On August 15, 1995, John flew with his family to Salt Lake City, Utah. Catholic Community Services was the agency assigned to resettle them in the new country. Catholic Community Services, like other voluntary agencies, had contracts with the US State Department and were paid to resettle refugees. Catholic Community Services found John and his family an apartment and a job assembling electronics that paid $5.25 an hour. Because John was working, he was not entitled to healthcare benefits for himself or his wife, only for their children. John's wife Rebecca collapsed three days after arriving in Salt Lake City. The hospital diagnosed her with a perforated ear drum caused from multiple untreated ear infections while living in the camps. Her ear drum required replacement, and the cost of the surgery was not covered by any program. To pay for it, John took three jobs. He would start his day early at the electronics assembly plant. By two o'clock he arrived at his second job at the Little Mother's Helper Company, where he collected and laundered dirty diapers and repackaged the clean ones. At night he worked in a chemical factory making kitty litter.

John managed to keep up the schedule for three months, but he still could not make ends meet. Additionally, there was no opportunity for John to continue his studies. Rebecca had an uncle in San Diego who implored them to come to California. The weather was similar to Southern Sudan, without extreme cold or heat, and the refugee benefits were thought to be better. In 1997, John packed up his family and moved to San Diego.

San Diego
Upon arrival, John enrolled in a City Heights adult school in the Adult Basic Education Program. After completing the program, John began to study for his General Educational Development (GED) test. At the same time, he enrolled in a Certified Nursing Assistant (CNA) program, working as an intern until he completed his GED. He finished his CNA training at San Diego City College and enrolled at National University, where he graduated with a Bachelor's degree in Psychology in 2006.

John performed his internship as a CNA caregiver at the Home of Guiding Hands in the small community of Santee, in eastern San Diego County. His six months of on-site training consisted of working with disabled children. At the conclusion of his internship, John was offered a part-time health education outreach position with Project Concern's New Americans program. He was accustomed to working in the community, and he would be able to talk about something near and dear to his heart, health education. Shortly after John started work with the New Americans program, he was offered another part-time community health position, this one focusing on mental health outreach through the ESSEA program at Alliance International University. Between the two jobs John was able to earn full-time pay. A short time later, ESSEA approached John to advise him that working both jobs constituted a conflict of interest. John was forced to choose between the two jobs, and he picked ESSEA because the program offered health insurance and benefits.

After six months, John's position with ESSEA changed to full-time. Shortly thereafter, however, the ESSEA grant expired, and the program was discontinued. John was laid off, and he and Rebecca were downhearted, fearing that they were right back where they started. Fortunately Rebecca's Uncle John, the one who had encouraged them to come to San Diego in the first place, was working in the economic development unit of La Maestra Community Health Centers. He introduced John to the staff, brought him along with him to health fairs, community events and every appropriate opportunity. John was offered full-time employment at La Maestra in 2006. John continued his studies and has obtained a certificate in Marriage and Family Therapy 2010, and is now able to provide counseling services in addition to health education.

John and Rebecca have eight children. Upon arriving to San Diego, they signed up for Section 8 public housing and were approved. John was laid off shortly after, so Rebecca started working but was laid off after three months. John wrote a letter notifying their Section 8 case worker of their job losses but received a document a few months later stating that they failed to notify Section 8 of the change in their work status, and had thus violated the rules. Although John took a copy of the letter they had sent into the Section 8 office, he was told that their case worker was no longer employed there, and the original letter was not in their file, so they were disqualified anyway. John and Rebecca have received no assistance since then and have found it very difficult to find safe, affordable housing with enough room for their large family. Many of the families in their community have gone through the same challenges.

Sudan Today
Present-day life in Southern Sudan is extremely difficult. There is plenty

of oil in Southern Sudan, but it is controlled by the north instead of the south. The COMP, *Comprehensive Peace Agreement*, negotiated in 2005 set a policy which stated that the south and the north would split the oil profits equally. In actuality, the north is estimated to receive closer to 75% of the overall revenues. No one in the south knows the precise number of barrels produced, or the sale price, because the north carefully controls it all. Sudan has 39 million people, 15 million of whom reside in the south. Starvation continues. Typhoid, cholera, smallpox and tuberculosis are common. Meningitis and HIV infections have increased dramatically.

Political negotiations continue, however slowly. The north, which is almost entirely Muslim, does not want to meet Darfur's requests. In the meantime, there can be no peace. The COMP gave Southern Sudan the right to govern itself for six years, until the year 2011. At that time, they will vote to decide if they wish to remain part of South Sudan, or secede altogether. Currently, the Sudanese Vice President is from the Dinka tribe. He is responsible for governing South Sudan, and because he is from the south, the people are content with the arrangement. They are a proud people, and remain hopeful in spite of their lack of infrastructure and capital.

The governments of Egypt, Iraq, and the Arab League of Nations continue to back the Northern Sudanese control over the country - in part because they are Muslim, and in part because it gives them greater access to the oil. Until the disbursement of oil and its profits are truly equitable between north and south, conflict will continue. John believes that the Northern government is massacring and intentionally starving out the people of South Sudan so that they can move in and claim all of their oil-rich land. While professing to be compliant in agreements for equality, John believes that the north blocks aid to the south. Disease is rampant, food is scarce and the killings continue. John can see no hope for equality or survival for the people of the south unless they secede from the greedy and power-starved north, taking their land and oil with them.

As a separate component of the 2005 COMP agreement, human trafficking - when Arabs from Northern Sudan would capture women, young girls and boys from Southern Sudan to sell in the Middle East - was halted. A rumor surfaced recently, accusing AIDS relief agencies of trying to sell children to European countries. John believes that these rumors were initiated by the Northern Sudanese government in an attempt to drive away outside assistance, allowing the target populations to perish sooner, and allowing the north to achieve their ultimate goal.

Hopes for the Future
John is hopeful that he will be in a better financial position three years from this writing. By then, he will have earned his Marriage and Family

Therapy certificate and license, and will be able to serve his community even greater. John believes that his eight children are gifts from God. They altered his life, making him a more joyful person. As a parent, his responsibility is to teach them well and to guide them: "What you do for others will come back to you," says John. John is hopeful that his children will continue the work he has started in their small community. He would like his children to help others, and through their works, perform God's mission here on earth. John was filled with pride when he heard his fifteen year old daughter tell a friend that she was very happy that her father was educated, allowing her to stay in school instead of going to work to help provide support for her family. She said, "My father is here. He is helping me complete school and be a better person." John believes that God helps us to be better people, helping others in return.

Regrets?
John has no real regrets. John wishes that his farm responsibilities had not caused him to begin his education so late, as it was difficult to catch up, beginning in the relief camps at age fifteen. It has been a long struggle, but one of which he is very proud.

John's Sudanese Family
John's aunt, who he refers to as "Mother", was able to leave Sudan and now resides in San Diego with one of John's sisters. John was able to sponsor a younger sister who is currently studying full time at college. She is married now, with children of her own. At the time of her sponsorship, John's sister was young and unmarried, meeting the criteria for immigration to the US. John's other sister unfortunately did not. She has been living in Ethiopia with her husband and children for the past ten years. They are not permitted to work. They rent a small room, supported exclusively by the money John sends to them every month for the past ten years. There is currently no hope of them being able to immigrate to the United States.

John's Church & Community Development
When John was seven years old, missionaries visited his village. Pupils of the original white missionaries, these Sudanese missionaries had brought Christianity to the Sudan. John and many of the young people were attracted by the teachings, as the missionaries brought drums, songs, and games along with the teachings of Jesus Christ. They called themselves Evangelists.

When the missionaries visited the next year, John knew he wanted to learn more about Jesus and his teachings. Only eight-years-old, John already understood that religion was more than play, and he was ready to take it seriously. John's father, whose god desired animal sacrifices, was not at all happy with his son's new-found religion. But slowly, over time, John managed to convince his father that Jesus was the true God, and his father accepted John's commitment. John was baptized at age ten, and he joined the church choir. He went on to become part of the teaching team and continued preaching the word of God until his arrival in the United States. John has been an active member of the College Center Covenant Evangelical Church since arriving in San Diego.

In 1998 the College Center Covenant Evangelical Church invited the Sudanese community of San Diego to join their congregation. The church and congregation continue to be extremely supportive of the Sudanese community, and can be counted on especially in times of crisis. A few years after joining the congregation, the Sudanese community was invited to conduct an additional service in their native language. John has many years of pastoral training and now preaches at the church each Sunday. He formed and leads a youth group, as well as a women's group on Wednesday evenings. John hopes to instill the desire to achieve and be fruitful in the community's youth. John's devotion to his community and church is strictly unpaid. His goal for his community is to make certain they know that God is real, that He is always with them, that He knows them, and has a plan for everyone. John believes that being a Christian is about helping others and assisting them in their spiritual development, always with hope for a better life. John says that Christians do not live forever, nor do they strive to obtain exaggerated riches. John remembers being chased by soldiers, walking for days with no certainty of survival, but he never wavered from his knowledge that God was with him. John soundly believes that God will continue showing him the way, providing opportunities for him and his fellow Christians. He says, "What God prefers for me, I will get it. It is just a matter of time." For John, God is constant while other things may come and go. During the ten years that he and his family have lived in the United States, John has faced many challenges, always getting through them with faith in the future. John says that nothing comes from God by accident. If we only listen, God will show us the way.

John serves God by serving his community. While preaching and mentoring in his church and attending school to earn his Marriage and Family Therapy certificate, John also works full-time at La Maestra Community Health Centers in the Job Training and Placement Unit. John also assists with translations for patient services. Having lived through so many challenges settling in San Diego, John acts as a guide to anyone having similar experiences. Unlike many in his community, John speaks fluent English, and is frequently called upon to aid in communication.

John's experiences growing up certainly contributed to his desire to help others. He grew up poor in a poor community. In the refugee camps John witnessed much suffering, motivating him to become a nurse. Most in the camps were illiterate, even in their own language. Many of these same refugees have come to this community here in San Diego. Because they can't speak English, they have difficulty finding a job or obtaining a driver's license. John created a program to teach the DMV manual to community members in their native language. He then convinced the California Department of Motor Vehicles to allow people to take the test in their own language.

John continues to be a source of major assistance to his community here in San Diego, and the needs are great. There are three tribes in San Diego, about 3,000 immigrants all together. Health, housing, jobs, and literacy remain the biggest challenges. At one time there were many more Sudanese immigrants residing in San Diego, but some have relocated to Omaha, Nebraska, to Minneapolis, Minnesota, to Des Moines, Iowa, and to Nashville Tennessee, in order to support their families. They work in meat factories which require no English literacy, just hard work. Some of those in San Diego have gone to work in the casinos, like the Lost Boys who speak English. Sadly, many of the Lost Boys have fallen prey to alcohol and other vices. They want to return to the Sudan to find wives, but until that happens, they will continue to be lost.

QUESTIONS

1. Where is Sudan in relationship to Africa?

2. How many tribes were in John's village? What were some of the differences between the tribes?

3. What is the hierarchal structure of the tribes? Where did women fit in the hierarchy?

4. Did the tribes have a history of conflict?

5. What is a sign of beauty in the Akobo tribe?

6. What religions existed in John's village when he was born?

7. What did the villages believe the power of the "evil eye" to be?

8. Are you familiar with other cultures that believe in the evil eye power?

9. What was John's position in his family? Was he revered because of his gender? Why?

10. What were the homes like? What effect did the value of livestock have on the configuration of the living quarter's structure?

11. Was education a right for all?

12. What were John's opportunities to become educated?

13. Why was John's father averse to John attending school?

14. Was there a connection between the value of a women and her ability to bear children?

15. What did the manhood ceremony represent?

16. How did the civil war in Sudan affect John's village? How old was John when it started?

17. What recourse did John have when the war reached his village?

18. Where was the first refugee camp where John lived for four years?

19. What were the living conditions like there?

20. What could have helped to control the diseases in the camp?

21. Where did the money come from to support the camp?

22. Where did John receive his basic education, elementary through high school?

23. How many refugees lived in the camp?

24. How many doctors were available to treat the refugees? Were they Sudanese doctors?

25. Were there enough medications for the refugees?

26. What duties did John have in his work in the refugee camp?

27. What happened to the Itang refugee camp when the host country, Ethiopia, had a change in government?

28. Where did John and his family go?

29. Where did John first meet Rebecca?

30. What were some of the challenges John faced in pursuing a marriage with Rebecca?

31. Where was the second refugee camp John went to? What were the living conditions like in the camp?

32. What was John's job there?

33. What discrepancies did John notice between the lists of medications and deaths provided to the U.N. and what he saw firsthand?

34. How many refugees lived in this camp?

35. What were the living quarters like in the camp?

36. How were the refugees treated in the camp? What were some of the risks in the camp for the refugees?

37. How were medications received for the refugee camp?

38. Why did John attempt to flee to Kenya with his family?

39. How did John and his family end up in the IFO refugee camp?

40. How many refugees lived in the IFO camp? Were did they come from?

41. How long did John live there?

42. What happened to the refugees who tested positive for contagious disease?

43. Who were the Lost Boys? How many Lost Boys were in the camp? How were they treated?

44. Why was their conditioning and training different?

45. When did John and his family get placed in the US? Who sponsored them?

46. Was John able to relax, removed from the war and the years in the refugee camps?

47. Did John's family receive healthcare benefits?

48. When his wife felt ill, how did John pay for the treatment?

49. How many jobs did John have in Salt Lake City?

50. Why did John decide to move his family to San Diego?

51. What work did John do in San Diego?

52. Why do you think John has continued to work in the community?

53. Why do you think control over Southern Sudan is sought after by the Northern Sudanese?

54. What support do the Northern Sudanese have and why?

55. What conditions in Sudan allow for human trafficking?

56. Does John have faith?

57. How does his belief in God affect his role in the community?

58. How does the Sudanese community in San Diego assist and support its people?

59. What work does John do now?

60. Was John given assistance during his acculturation in the U.S?

61. How were John and his family helped by the public housing system in San Diego?

62. What are some of John's voluntary activities?

63. What are some of John's hopes for the future?

64. What are some of the differences and challenges that the Lost Boys face in the US? Do they fit into the Sudanese refugee communities?

65. What characteristics does John have as a human being?

66. Do you think that John views himself as an American?

John Kang's Story

Editor's Note: La Maestra Community Health Centers staff nominated John Kang, (referred to as "Uncle John" in John Kueck's story), and his family for the "Brighten a Life" story in the San Diego Union Tribune. The nomination was accepted and the reporter, Ozzie Roberts, followed and interviewed John Kang for two days to produce the 2001 story. Mr. Roberts wrote a follow-up article following John Kang's death in 2006.

John Kang spent much of his life in a refugee camp in civil war-ravaged Sudan. Faced with religious persecution from an early age, John and his family found it nearly impossible to observe their Christian traditions. "When I was a kid – 7 years old – I knew I wouldn't be given an education if I said I was a Christian, and I knew that they were cutting off the heads of people who wouldn't give up their belief," said Kang in a 2001 interview with the San Diego Union Tribune. Kang had lived in refugee camps for more than 33 years, noting, "There's nothing good in refugees' camps – people live only to die there." Kang's mother had died in a refugee camp, and his father was killed in route.

John and his wife, Mary Thanypieny, relocated to San Diego with eight small children as part of an international refugee resettlement program in 1994, which included some 8,000 Sudanese.

Having spent all or most of their lives in refugee camps, many Sudanese immigrants arrived in their new country with little or no schooling, and could not speak or understand English. Others, like Kang, found that their education and skills did not translate to employment in the US Kang studied and practiced veterinary medicine for sixteen years in and around his native Sudan, where a man's life and livelihood depended upon the health of his domestic animals. He continued to practice medicine in the Kenyan and Ethiopian refugee camps where he lived for 33 years. But when he arrived in the US, his credentials were insufficient to find employment in his field.

Recognizing that more than a half-century's devastation to his country made the option of return for he and his fellow refugees hopeless, Kang founded the Sudanese Community Association. The local non-profit organization was staffed entirely by volunteers who counseled Sudanese refugees, helping them to establish connections and adjust to the challenges of life in the new homeland. "In Africa, we couldn't think of anything but a struggle for life – I can't get away from that thinking," continued Kang in the Union Tribune interview. "And that's why I started the association." Members of Kang's organization endeavored to bring the community together, and to improve the conditions of their daily lives.

In 1998, after having failed to obtain full-time employment in more than two dozen attempts, Kang went to work for La Maestra Community Health Centers in City Heights. Speaking five languages, Kang's position as intake case manager also included translator, teacher, counselor, and just about anything else that was needed. Kang had become familiar with La Maestra when clinic workers assisted him in a desperate search to find affordable housing for his large family.

In 2005, Kang received an invitation from the Sudanese Delegation asking him to participate in major peace negotiations between Northern and Southern Sudan. Having been a part of previous negotiations which produced Anayna I, Anayna II and the SPLA, Kang was integral to the process. In spite of concerns from fellow employees and family members about the indiscriminate bombings in the area, as well as kidnapping and killing of the influential delegates traveling to the Sudan to be part of this peace process, Kang took leave from his work at La Maestra and traveled to Sudan. After a long negotiation period, an agreement called the Comprehensive Peace Agreement was reached.

A month and a half after his departure, Kang returned home to San Diego, exhausted, but pleased that an agreement had been struck. As time went on, however, his former energy failed to return. Kang went in for a physical exam and was referred to a specialist who referred him for a liver biopsy. Kang was diagnosed with Hepatitis B and informed that the disease had destroyed his liver. Recommended for a liver transplant, Kang continued to lose weight while he waited for a suitable donor. Just three months later, John Kang, who had done so much for so many, died at the age of 47. Although his care in the hospital for the two weeks leading up to his death included dialysis, a respirator, and medications for his liver, the management of his case through Medi-Cal up to that time literally fell through the cracks. His name had never made it to the liver transplant list, and there had been no follow-up from the private provider, a renal specialist, regarding the condition of his liver. Kang was survived by his wife and nine children.

Following Kang's death, life for Mary Thanypieny and her children became more uncertain than ever before. Her husband of 23 years had just died, as had her baby girl, born three months premature. But then something miraculous began to occur. In and around the Sudanese community where she and her husband had lived and worked, news of John's death began to circulate. In addition to his work at La Maestra, Kang had served as a pastor for the Sudanese Fellowship at College Center Community Church. People showed up at Thanypieny's door with toys and clothing, enough for every member of the household. They brought food and money; they paid bills, including the rent. "People put their hands together and they helped my family," Thanypieny said in a 2006 interview with the San Diego Union Tribune. "There are people out there who know, when a problem like this happens, what's behind it, and they come together for those in need. I just want to thank them all. God will bless them. I believe that."

Following Kang's death, La Maestra submitted a proposal for assistance to the Bollinger Foundation, a nonprofit organization created to provide financial assistance to families of economic development, community development, and public housing workers, for the education and support of children who have lost a parent or guardian. The proposal was approved, and an assistance grant in the amount of $17,000 was awarded to the Kang family, allowing the elder children to continue their studies in lieu of quitting to work full-time to support the family. Kang's cousin, John Kueck, continues to watch over the Kang family. The family is involved in the church groups that Kueck coordinates and, as his "Uncle John" had helped him, John Kueck felt honored to reciprocate.

QUESTIONS

1. Where was John born?

2. What religion did John's family practice?

3. How were Christians treated in John's country?

4. What happened to John's parents?

5. When did John arrive in San Diego?

6. What profession did John have in Sudan? Was he able to practice this profession in the US?

7. How many years did John have to live in the refugee camp?

8. What community organization did John start in San Diego? Why did he start this organization?

9. Where did John find employment in San Diego? What was his position there?

10. Why did John return to Sudan in 2005? What risks did he take in accepting this mission?

11. What role did John play in the peace process?

12. What health condition did John develop?

13. How old was John when he died? What family members did he leave?

14. How was his family able to survive his death?

15. At which church did John serve as a pastor?

16. Which foundation stepped up to help John's family?

17. How is John remembered in his community?

Savanh's Story

Childhood

Savanh was the youngest of six children born to Vene and Sene. She was only eleven months old when her mother, Vene, died of dysentery. The oldest child, a boy, died at age four. Savanh and her four sisters continued to live with her father until the sisters married. Her father was a farmer. He grew rice and raised cows and buffalo. Her father then became a Buddhist Monk and went to live at the Temple.

At age seven, Savanh went to live with her second oldest sister, named La, her sister's husband, Som, and their two children. Later they had four more children. La stayed home and cared for the children and cooked while Som worked as a farmer and fisherman. During the rainy season from June to mid-October he would plant rice, and from mid-October to December he would fish, as there was still a lot of rain and the fish were plentiful. The dry season started in December and Som would cut wood to sell as firewood. He also had cows, buffalo and chickens. Both her sister and brother-in-law were very nice to Savanh, treating her as their child, as she was only five years older than their oldest child.

Savanh's duty was to watch her niece and nephew and play with them. This was a serious job as there were constant dangers of being abducted or killed in the woods where warring parties hid. Savanh remembers being terrified at night as a child, listening to gunfire in the mountains and forests between the monarchy of King Sisavang Vong and the Independent Party backed by the Vietnamese government.

When Savanh was born in 1944, Laos was still a French colony. There was constant conflict between the two political powers. In 1945, the Japanese invaded Laos and the French were run out. The conflict intensified as more powers were struggling for control of the country. The Japanese were defeated and left. Once more the French moved in. The economy continued to be unstable and there was ongoing poverty throughout the land.

The family lived in a separate house and they owned their own land. Savanh considered her family to be middle-class. She had a few shirts and skirts to wear, and one sweater. She remembers always being cold and constantly suffering from a runny nose. But because her family owned land and they always had rice to eat, along with some fish or vegetables or chicken, that classified her family as middle-class. There were many less fortunate who did not have enough food to eat. She would see her father frequently, as it was the custom each week to take an offering of food to the monks at the Temple. All of her family lived in Vang Vieng, a suburb of Vientiane, the capital of Laos. The town is situated in front of the Nam Song River. *Nam* means river in Laotian. It was lovely, with mountains in the background. The town was small and everyone knew each other. The town faced the river, running lengthwise along its bank. There were plenty of fish and the children enjoyed swimming among them in the clear water of the river. The houses were all built upon high stilts to avoid flooding during the rainy season. Some people kept their livestock under the house. The shape of the houses was like two connected squares, with pointed roofs. Savanh remembers the peaceful feeling of stepping out of her house, looking at the clear green river water and the mountains on the other side, both covered with a fine mist. The air smelled of wildflowers.

Savanh attended public school, operated by the government. There were no private schools. Elementary school was six years, followed by another four years of high school. Savanh completed elementary school and two years of high school. At that time, there was only one elementary school in the town. If adults wanted to become literate they went to the Temple.

Savanh was accepted into the Teacher's College, in Dongdok, about fifty miles away from her hometown of Vang Vieng, where she was trained for one year and received her certificate as an elementary school teacher. Her first assignment was to teach in Vientiane. She lived with her aunt, her mother's sister. Savanh later returned to Vang Vieng, where she taught at the elementary school and again lived with her sister and family.

Marriage
Savanh attended her cousin's wedding, where she met her future husband, Khom. He was a first lieutenant in the military, stationed in Vientiane. They exchanged letters over the course of one year, as there were no telephones. They were not permitted to meet or go out as it was forbidden. Khom proposed marriage and came to formally ask for her hand in marriage. Savanh always considered herself an independent thinker, which was rare for women at that time. She knew that the arranged marriages she had seen were not always successful. One example was her sister, who was matched up with a man that had no family and no financial obligations, and thus was considered to be a good match. Her sister did not know him and

would hide from him after they were married. Savanh realized that they did not love each other and wanted something different for herself. She knew that her relationship with Khom was different and that they cared for each other.

It was customary for the bride's family to ask for a high dowry from the groom, even if they never collected the whole amount. It was a point of pride to be able to tell others that their daughter's husband had given a large dowry for their daughter, implying that she was very special. Savanh was worried about this, so she asked him how much money he had. He said that he had saved a modest amount but could borrow more if needed. Savanh did not want him to borrow any money which they would have to repay later. So she spoke to her family and asked them not to ask for a high dowry amount and explained why. Savanh's family agreed to ask for a modest amount. Her father's main concern was where the couple would live. Khom's family lived far away. Khom assured Savanh's family that they would not move to his family's village but would stay somewhere within the vicinity of Savanh's hometown or in Vientiane, depending on his assignment. Savanh's father made Khom promise that if he were to be assigned to a faraway place, he would return Savanh to her family until he was relocated closer. He agreed, and the blessing was given.

Savanh planned the wedding with her family and friends. Since she was a teacher she knew everyone. Khom was not able to help as he was still in Vientiane. The day before the wedding, he arrived in Vang Vieng with fifteen of his soldiers to help. The wedding and reception ceremony followed Lao tradition.

The eve of the wedding was busy with cooking and entertaining guests at Savanh's sister's home. Friends and family came to visit, eat, or help in the preparations. On the morning of the wedding, Savanh dressed herself with the traditional bridal garments, called *sinh*. Her blouse and skirt were of homemade black silk woven with threads of green and gold silk. Her hair was pulled up into a bun, called *khamkao* (*pronounced "camcow"*), and decorated with gold chains. Once dressed, she sat inside her room waiting for the procession.

Khom, his aunt and his soldiers formed a parade, carrying a big silver bowl filled with the dowry. They also carried trays of food and wine. According to custom, a special couple was stationed at the door of her house, blocking the entrance. It was important that this special couple had only been married once, never having previous marriages. It symbolized the importance that Savanh's marriage last forever. Those preparing the pa basi, the wedding ceremony centerpieces, also had to fit this requirement of having been married only once.

Once Khom and the procession reached Savanh's door, the couple asked Khom, "Why are you coming here today?" Khom's group then answered, "Because we know that you have a good daughter, a beautiful daughter, and we have a good son. We would like to join them in marriage to unite our two families." Savanh's side then asked, "Are you sure that you want to be a good son?" "Yes," said Khom. According to tradition, this dialog between the bride's family and the groom's family can continue for some time depending on the size of the groups involved, with humor and laughter as part of the ritual.

The couple at Savanh's door then asked, "What are you bringing with you today? Do you have the money to open this door?" At that point Khom said, "Yes, I do," presenting the dowry, and the special couple blocking the door offered the end of a gold chain for Khom to hold and led him into the house. Khom then sat down in the middle of the room, next to the pa basi centerpieces. The special couple then went to bring Savanh into the room and sat her down on the floor next to Khom and the two large wedding centerpieces.

The Wedding Ceremony: Basi
The bride and groom sat next to each other on the floor by the pa basi centerpieces, two huge silver bowls filled with flowers and strings. The wedding officiator began by wishing the new couple many blessings and then described how couples should behave and the essentials of a good marriage. Both Savanh and Khom had strings tied around their wrists. The strings represented joining together and keeping a good spirit in the body. They asked for their families' blessings and the ceremony finished. The reception followed with traditional food and a small live band of local musicians. Everybody was happy, talking, dancing, eating and celebrating. The reception lasted for six or seven hours. The tradition does not include a honeymoon. The new couple helped to clean up and return all of the many borrowed items which had made the ceremony possible.

"The Hardest Time in My Life Began"
Savanh and Khom moved to Vientiane and had three children. Khom was promoted to Captain. In 1975, the Communist regime took control of Laos and the suffering began. The Communists had built up momentum starting in Russia, spreading into Vietnam, then Laos and Cambodia.

Savanh's husband had remained a Captain and the couple was disappointed when all of his comrades were promoted to Majors except him. Actually, this was a blessing in disguise. Once in power, the first thing that the Communists did was immediately remove all of the Majors and send them to detention camps far away in the mountains north of Laos. The excuse given was that the Majors needed to attend two week long "re-education seminars" which were really jails. King Sisavang Watana was sitting in the monarchy at the time, the son of King Sisavang Vong who reigned during the time when Savanh was born. The Communists removed King Watana, along with his wife, children, and family, sending them to a town in the mountains called Viengxay where they were starved to death. All of the leaders were also tricked into leaving, thinking that they would be given orientation about the new regime, but instead were killed.

Savanh's husband was taken to a re-education seminar as well but fared better because he was sent to a camp about two hours from Vientiane. He stayed there for two years, unable to communicate with Savanh. This was a very difficult time for Savanh as she was the sole supporter of her three children. At that time, her eldest boy was eight years old, her daughter four years old and her youngest boy two years old. She would take her baby boy with her to work where she had been promoted to school principal. Her eldest boy stayed home, watching his sister and helping Savanh with the household. All domestic help was forbidden by the Communists. Everyone had to take care of their own families.

Food was scarce. The Communists told the farmers that they had to work in teams. Instead of becoming more productive, the effect was the opposite. Working harder and producing more was not rewarded; all farmers shared alike. This caused dissent among farmers as some worked harder than others but still received the minimum. The team approach was not successful, making food scarcer and more expensive.

Music was removed from all of the radio stations and replaced with Communist propaganda. Songs that had any reference to feelings or that had words about love were despised and banned. Any entertainment on television was stopped, replaced with stories about farmers and agriculture. So there was no entertainment and the stress was incredible.

Savanh did not know if she would ever see her husband again. She could hear her friends crying at night, unable to bear the anguish of having their families torn apart and left without any hope for better times. In this oppressive atmosphere, despair was rampant. Savanh would pass her friends on the street and they would just cry together, not being able to say anything. Any complaints overheard were punished severely.

The Escape
Finally Savanh's husband was released him for a family visit and he returned to Vientiane. Upon his return, Savanh and Khom immediately planned their escape. They did not share their plans with their families, not because they didn't trust them, but they were worried that it would place the relatives' lives in danger or that the information would leak out

to the authorities.

At that time, Savanh's youngest niece and nephew were living with them because her sister and brother-in-law had been sent to one of the re-education seminars and had not returned. Savanh had no idea what would happen, or if they were ever going to return, so she kept her niece and nephew with her. Five years later they were released. They had survived working seven days a week clearing the jungles with no tools. During that time, they were given no change of clothing. They had to make do sewing patches on their clothing. No medicines were available, so they relied on herbs from the jungles to cure their illnesses. Many died from fevers. They returned home to find their two youngest children gone. The brother-in-law suffered mental disturbances and was never the same again.

One day, Savanh took her children and her niece and nephew to school, with money and gold sewn into their clothing. She told them that they were going on a field trip. Her husband arranged with one of his friends to rent a boat which would take them across the Mekong River into Thailand. The family dressed in very tattered clothes, disguising themselves as poor farmers, and walked through the fields toward the river. The Mekong River was only two kilometers from where they lived. However, it was impossible to take a direct route to the river as soldiers were patrolling constantly. Some escapees had to take very roundabout paths through the woods, the jungle and the rice fields, adding another 30 to 50 kilometers to this part of the escape route. Others continued to trek up to 200 kilometers before reaching a safe place along the river to cross. Unfortunately, many fell prey to thieves who robbed or killed them.

Savanh and her family finally made it to the river crossing. The boat ride was terrifying. Many others had attempted this crossing, only to be shot by either the Communist soldiers on the Laotian side or the Thai soldiers on the other side of the river. The boat captain who took Savanh and her family across knew how to navigate them away from the dangers and they reached Thailand. There they reported to the Thai government that they had escaped, were put into the jail for three days, and then were given a document which allowed them to enter the first of two "detention" camps run by the Thai government. This was the first step before even being able to register their names with the United Nations.

Savanh, her husband, their three children, and Savanh's niece and nephew were sent to the first detention camp. In recalling the conditions and experiences of this camp, Savanh says, "I do not want to think about that because then I do not want to eat". There were approximately 100 people in a space of 400 square feet. They had to eat, sleep, stand and defecate in that same space. There was absolutely no privacy and no room to breathe. Pre-packaged food consisting of rice and fish was distributed once per day. This was not enough, so many starved. Those that had brought some money with them could buy extra food. The dilemma was that if the guards suspected that a family had money they would use all kinds of excuses to keep them in this camp and not move them on, so they could extract more money from them. The alternative was to starve.

The guards were very abusive. They would select people to pick on and beat them, verbally abuse them or worse, remove them from the camp and they would never be seen again. They did this as an example to instill fear in the detainees, so nobody would ask any questions or complain.

Savanh and her family stayed two weeks at the first camp. Then they were transferred to the second detention camp, also run by the Thai government. This camp was much bigger, about 20,000 square feet, and held at least 1,000 people. The conditions were equally poor. Food was scarce; there were no blankets and no mats to sleep on. The abuse continued there - the guards would usually select men to pick on and abuse. Occasionally they would remove young girls for the night, rape them and return them to the detention camp the next day. Nobody would say anything, as survival of the family was priority. Those moving on would sell their blankets to those just arriving. Savanh began to despair at ever being able to reach the refugee camp where they would be allowed to register their names with the United Nations.

Nong Khai Refugee Camp
Finally Savanh and her family were sent to the refugee camp called Nong Khai. The camp was run by the Thai government and sponsored by UNESCO. There were thirty to forty thousand refugees in this camp. When Savanh and her family arrived, they were told to stay on a small platform with no walls, just a grass-covered roof. They stood there looking around, totally lost, not knowing what was going to happen. People walked by looking at them and they tried to recognize someone. Savanh cries as she remembers the feeling of being lost and unaware of what to do. Luckily, she found a cousin who took her and her family into her small room. They stayed with her cousin until they found and bought a hut from a family that was moving on.

The United Nations was not aware that the huts were sold and resold. The only refugees who were able to get a hut without paying were the very first ones to arrive at the camp. The inspectors who would visit had no idea of the reality of what went on in the camp. They would visit one family who would answer questions with replies fabricated to satisfy the inspectors. The reality was that the refugees were treated very badly. The guards abused their power and degraded the refugees, verbally, physically, and mentally abusing them. The refugees were not treated as human beings. The guards did not care who the person was or where they came from. Church groups would sometimes come to visit, but concentrated on helping the orphans and a few families. Camp life was totally void of respect for anyone. Social class and age did not matter. In Lao culture, the elderly are revered, but not so in the camp.

The refugees received a weekly stipend of rice, and sometimes vegetables or chicken. It was a meager amount and families were starving. Some were lucky enough to have brought money or gold with them so they were able to supplement their stipend of food with what was sold in the market inside the camp. Savanh bought material and her friend sewed, so they were able to sell clothing to make money. Khom spoke English, which enabled him to work, earning one dollar a day, with the United States' Immigration Service to translate for those applying for refugee status in the United States. This barely supported Savanh's family in the camp.

Because the huts were so close together, it was impossible to ever be at peace. Arguing and fighting could be heard constantly. Savanh's hut was covered by a grass roof which had to be replaced each year. It was the size of a small office, about five by ten feet, for seven people to live in. They lived there for one and a half years which was considered to be a short time. Her children did not go to school as it cost money for them to attend. She taught them lessons in their hut but they were all very distracted and afraid because of the environment that surrounded them day and night. Savanh was terrified of going outside of her hut, not wanting to see and hear the abuse or risk experiencing more of it. She says, "I felt so much hurt because of the abuse so I did not want to go out of my area to risk getting this treatment." Some of the refugees ventured outside the camp to look for work. The only positive comment that Savanh said about the camp was that it was the first time she heard music since 1975 when the Communists took control of Laos and removed it from the airways.

In order to be eligible for refugee asylum, the applicants had to demonstrate that they had qualifications and a sponsor. Savanh's husband, Khom, had been a capitan in the Laotian army and worked with the US Immigration Service in the camps as a translator, so they met the qualifications. They were sponsored by the World Church in Connecticut, where Khom had come two times for community leadership training.

Of course, Savanh was worried about what would happen to them but says, "I just closed my eyes and knew that whatever happens is better than what we came out of." At least she and her husband and children were alive and together. This was not the case for many others. People routinely "disappeared". Others were maimed by the beatings from the guards, and some never qualified for refugee status. Those unfortunates remained in the camp for many years until the camp was closed and then were transferred to a city in Thailand. Some returned home to Laos only to be executed as punishment for their defection. Those who made it back home, and managed to avoid being killed, found that their property in Laos had been confiscated and their families who remained in Laos had been punished for aiding their escape to Thailand. After Savanh and her family escaped, the Communists visited her sister and tried to hold her responsible for Savanh's defection. Luckily, her sister had been in the hospital on the day that Savanh left, so the guards could not prove that the sister had in any way assisted Savanh. They tried to confiscate Savanh's house but the sister and father said that it was theirs and they had just rented it to Savanh. Her father remained in the Temple. The Communists discouraged religion of any kind and would criticize those who had faith in God. They would stop people on their way to the Temple and say, "Why are you going there? It is a waste of time!" Or, "Better spend your time doing something productive like working."

A New Life in the United States
Savanh and her family arrived to Connecticut in December. It was bitterly cold and they had their first experience with snow. They had no idea what to expect and there were no organizations to assist them in the resettlement process. Their sponsors took them into their home and told Savanh that she would be working in the childcare unit of the church and Khom would start working in a factory. Everything was so alien to them. They had no family or friends in Connecticut. Savanh had one cousin who lived in Minnesota and another in California. Both cousins urged her to move in with them. Her first question to them was, "Does it snow where you live?" That determined where the family would relocate. The sponsor bought them the bus tickets to Los Angeles where they arrived and moved in with her cousin.

The bus ride was very disturbing to Savanh. It seemed to take forever and she was terrified that her family would be separated. In New York City, her husband had suggested that he go and find some food for them. She begged him not to leave them, even for a few minutes, and asked that they all go together everywhere. She spoke no English and did not know what to do if he got lost or if the bus left without him. This was a huge concern. However, Savanh was happy to be reunited with her cousin and to have the opportunity at starting a new life in their new country.

Right away, she saw that many things were different in the United States. The shapes of the houses were different; the environment was totally unlike anything she had ever experienced. She did not want to go outside the apartment because she did not understand a word of English and was afraid of getting lost or someone talking to her and not being able to understand. Her husband Khom was also hesitant to venture out, but was more confident since he spoke English.

Khom found a job as a teacher's aide in an English as a Second Language program. He earned $3.88 per hour. As refugees, they qualified for welfare, so they applied and this helped a lot. Savanh asked her husband to inquire at the school if she could attend and bring her three and half year old toddler with her. They agreed, so Savanh began learning English and venturing out of her apartment. The other two children were in school as well. She attended class during the morning and afternoon, determined to learn English. Then she went for training for electronic assembly.

A school counselor asked Savanh if she would be willing to work as an interpreter at a medical clinic. She was hesitant because her English was still not fluent. The counselor convinced her that her vocabulary was sufficient for basic translation. So she began working part time at a community clinic. She translated for a Pilipino physician who had been to Laos and was familiar with the culture.

Savanh began to build her self-confidence and focus on helping others. She quickly became familiar with the families in the Lao community and their problems. Once she learned the system at the community clinic, she was empowered to help in other ways, like giving support to other Laotians who were facing challenges of acculturation similar to what she had experienced. Health education about family planning and HIV prevention were two of the health programs which Savanh was involved in at the clinic. Most of the Lao community is Buddhist. Buddhism does not condone killing life, so abortions were not an option for many. Savanh felt that the community became more receptive to birth control after some years in the United States.

Her husband Khom has also been very involved in the Lao community and served as President on the Board of Directors for the Laotian Community of Southern California, and later as the Vice President of the Lao Veterans of Southern California. There are approximately 20,000 Laotians living in southern California. He has worked as a certified court interpreter and a counselor at a community-based organization. During the course of his work, he has been able to meet and assist many Lao families, guiding them to resources and giving them support. This encouraged Khom to strengthen the Laotian associations and form the Lao Cultural Association to better serve their community. A huge challenge in that organization's development has been funding. Community-based organizations would often ask for letters of support and promise to include the Laotian Cultural Association in the grant budget to allow them to build the infrastructure needed to provide support services like translation, transportation and help in finding work for their community members. Unfortunately, when the grants were awarded, very few of the dollars made their way to the Lao community as had been promised.

Many of the Lao refugees were placed in jobs without adequate training so they were unable to keep those jobs. Access to economic development is still a challenge for the community. Access to healthcare for the Lao community was and still is a challenge in California. Many do not understand or accept that they have chronic diseases. They still need a lot of health education. More cultural liaisons are needed to work in the community, as they are from the community and more trusted than outsiders. There are many physical and mental health issues which have not been sufficiently addressed. Many Laotians have post traumatic shock syndrome. For years, Khom would have horrible nightmares, screaming and kicking in his sleep, reliving the trauma and torture he experienced. Savanh also suffered years of dreaming about being lost or killed. She would often dream of the people back in Laos asking her, "how will you ever be able to return here?"

Savanh's job at the community clinic became full time and she continued there for seventeen years. Her skills and experience grew. The clinic moved her into the billing department, but in 1998 they reorganized and let Savanh go. She then heard about another community clinic, a grassroots community organization, which was also serving the Laotian community. She went to search for a job there and was hired. She has been very happy at being part of the service delivery system and continues to provide health education, translation, social services and referrals for many low-income patients.

Savanh remembers a case about ten years ago of a Lao woman who came to the clinic. The patient entered on the back of a neighbor. She had to be carried as she had no arms and stubs for legs. The woman complained that the cement was so hot that it burned her stumps when she tried to walk outside so she would wait to be carried on someone's back. The doctor was horrified at the lack of assistance that this woman had suffered. He asked how long she had been in the United States. She said five years. So for five years this woman could have been receiving assistance from disability programs and a wheelchair and many other services. She only was able to eat because neighbors prepared food and fed her. During the visit at the clinic, Savanh was able to refer the patient to disability programs and help her apply. This is an example of how refugees can fall through the gap, not being referred to programs for which they qualify. They do not know about such programs, much less how to apply for them or if they are eligible.

Among the refugee community, there are some who were guards and abused people back in the refugee camps and in Laos. I ask Savanh how she feels about this, having to live among those who took part in the torment of others. She replies that they are all surviving here and make the best of the situation, even though it is a constant reminder of those horrible times, and that perhaps they were also tortured themselves. That is a good point. Oftentimes the torturers were victims themselves in the beginning.

Family Life in Los Angeles
As her children grew up and began to date, both Savanh and her husband were concerned. When their son told them that he was dating a non-Laotian they really were worried. They told him that they had no prejudice against other cultures but did not see how they would be able to have much in common with other traditions or beliefs – the customs, the food, and the language would all be different. They encouraged their son to date Lao girls. He married a Lao woman, had three children and then divorced. He remarried, this time to a Vietnamese girl, and had another child. After the initial shock, both Savanh and her husband accepted the situation and grew very fond of their Vietnamese daughter-in-law, who is raising the other three children as well. Their daughter married an American whose father is of German descent and whose mother is Pilipino. Savanh and Khom had more acculturation challenges, but have always been supportive of their children's choices in marriage. It was very different than what they were accustomed to but they were willing to change their outlook and widen it to include other cultures into their family. They understand that their children grew up in this new environment and did not want to interfere with their happiness or successes.

Savanh's niece and nephew lived with them in Los Angeles until they got married. Both graduated from high school and work as electronic technicians. They both married Laotians and each have two children. Their children call Savanh "Grandma". Savanh and Khom raised them as their own children, including them in every family activity and event. Savanh is so happy that she was able to give them the love and nurturing that she received from her own sister when she went to live with her at a young age. She was able to repay her sister and brother-in-law for the kindness they showed to her as a child. Recently, the niece and nephew traveled back to Laos to see their parents after many years. It was a blessing for all.

It took years for Savanh and her husband to overcome the underlying fears that followed them for years under the Communist regime in Laos, during their escape, in the detention and refugee camps, and then with the challenges they faced in moving to a totally new environment. Stress in their new country was high but nothing compared to the situations in the past which threatened their survival. They are still governed by fear of the Communists in Laos as reports from the United States go back to the Lao government. If the Lao government suspects that any insurgent activities are being developed by expatriates, they punish the relatives who still live in Laos. Savanh, Khom and others living in the US are very mindful and fearful of retaliation against their families in Laos. They are afraid to speak openly about the conditions there.

Savanh is grateful that she and her family are alive and her children are settled in their new country. She is proud of her accomplishments and her work in helping others, and says that she is happy "because others can depend on me to help them". Both she and Khom spend their free time helping in the community. It gives them a strong sense of reward and accomplishment to stay involved and take part in positive changes for the many needy people who still cannot access healthcare and jobs. Savanh and Khom are also dedicated to preserving the Lao culture for the next generations who are born in the United States. The dilemma is how to assimilate without losing their culture, language and traditions. Savanh likes to spend time with children and tell them stories about her life in Laos and her experiences in coming to this country, in the hopes that they will carry forth this knowledge and it will give them a sense of history and pride in their heritage. Savanh has strong faith. She visits the temple on religious occasions and knows that her faith has helped her throughout her life.

Looking Back

In 1997, Savanh became a citizen of the United States. The first thing she did was book a trip to Laos to see her father and family. She was among the first twenty Laotians to visit Laos as a United States citizen. Many warned her not to go and were afraid for her but she was determined to make the trip. When she arrived in Laos, the American Consul greeted her, gave her his card and said, "If you need any help or if you feel threatened in any way, call me. You are the fourth one to come back to visit." Savanh spent one month in Laos.

She was so happy to see her family but at the same time so saddened by the conditions. The communists are still in power. Health care is absolutely minimal – there is no preventative care, only emergency cases are dealt with at the hospital. The medical equipment is very old. The government of Laos says that there is free healthcare but in reality, there are not enough medicines or supplies to take care of the people. The few who have money travel to Thailand for operations. Many people came to visit Savanh and ask about their relatives in the United States. Having no idea of the vastness of the United States, they would ask her, "Do you know my brother?" Savanh would ask, "Where does he live?" to which they would answer "New York." She sadly explained that she could give no information on the relatives they so desperately were seeking information about, since they lived so far from her home in Los Angeles. The concept was difficult, as Laos is such a small country compared to the United States.

The Lao government did not allow her to bring a camera into the country. They asked her how much money she was bringing in and inspected her belongings. They compared what she had brought in to what she was leaving with. They didn't mind that she brought money and gifts into the country but would not permit her to take anything out. She returned home to Los Angeles, knowing in her heart that she could never go back to live in Laos. She had adapted to her new country and new way of life and her children were settled with their own families. The Lao refugees who stayed in Thailand have never been accepted as equal members of the community. They have intermarried with the Thai people but have yet to gain equal status. This remains an issue so much that today there are many "volunteers" living in Thailand who are waiting to return to Laos. Savanh is grateful that she and her family were adopted by the United States and have equal rights and opportunities for her children to study and pursue careers.

Savanh regrets that she was not able to further her education and obtain a degree. However, she does not question the life she was given. She feels so proud of herself and of the work she continues to do, helping others. During her trips back to Laos her family treats her as a very special, respected person. She is honored because of the role she took on as mother to her sister's children, raising them in the United States and for her work here. Her father brags to everyone that Savanh is a doctor. She tries to explain to him that she is not a doctor but he says that it makes no difference because she works with doctors and helps others become well. They have heard of Savanh's activities in the Lao community and the respect that she and Khom have earned.

Savanh and other Laotians dream of returning to help rebuild Laos but realize that there is no chance of this happening while the current government is in power. It is believed that the Communists take their orders from Vietnam. Until this changes, there is little hope of Laos flourishing again.

QUESTIONS

1. Where was Savanh born? Who raised her?

2. What was Savanh's father's profession?

3. What education did Savanh pursue?

4. How did Savanh meet her husband-to-be? How was their courtship carried out?

5. What was the traditional acceptable dowry?

6. What are some of the Lao wedding customs?

7. Does the weeding tradition include a honeymoon?

8. When did the Communist regime take over Laos? How did this regime gain its momentum to invade Laos?

9. What were the re-education seminars?

10. What was the fate of King Sisavong Watana?

11. What happened to Savanh's husband?

12. How did Savanh manage to survive under the Communist regime?

13. What was life like for many under Communist rule?

14. How were complaints handled by the Communist rulers?

15. Why did the "team" system fail for the farmers?

16. How did Savanh and her family escape from Laos?

17. What were some of the perils crossing the Mekong River?

18. What happened when Savanh and her family reached Thailand? Were they welcomed?

19. Describe the first "detention camp" where Savanh and her family were sent.

20. Who controlled the second detention camp where Savanh and her family were sent?

21. What were some of the atrocities suffered by Laotian refugees there?

22. Were Savanh and the other refugees able to register with the United Nations?

23. Which refugee camp did Savanh and her family end up in? How many refugees were there?

24. What were some of the feelings that Savanh and her family experienced upon arrival to the refugee camp?

25. How did the refugees obtain a hut in the camp?

26. How were the refugees treated in the camp?

27. How long did Savanh and her family live in the camp? How did they manage to survive?

28. Who sponsored Savanh and her family to live in the US? What happened to refugees who could not find a sponsor?

29. Was Savanh's family back in Laos punished for Savanh's escape?

30. What is the main religion for Laotians?

31. What were the Communist rulers' views on religion and faith in God?

32. What was life like for Savanh and her family in Connecticut?

33. What was the trip from Connecticut to California like? What were some of Savanh and her family's fears?

34. What challenges did Savanh and her family face in California?

35. What was Savanh's first job in California?

36. What are some of the cultural differences that Savanh and her husband have had to reconcile?

37. How have Savanh's niece and nephew benefited from being raised by Savanh and her husband?

38. Does Savanh see a connection between her sister raising her and then her raising her niece and nephew?

39. Both Savanh and her husband suffer from Post Traumatic Stress. What activities do they get involved in to help their community and other refugees and immigrants?

40. How do you feel about Savanh returning to visit Laos? What do you think she was feeling?

41. Do Savanh and her husband still have fears of retribution for themselves and their families back in Laos?

42. According to Savanh, what change in Laos must happen in order for living conditions to improve?

43. Do you think that Savanh and her family are Americans?

44. In what ways do you think Savanh and her family are grateful to be in their new country?

45. What do they contribute to their new country?

QUESTIONS FOR REFLECTION

Growing Up - Life in the Home Country

1. What was the family unit structure like for each story? What were the family roles of the survivor, and of his or her parents, siblings, and relatives?

2. What was the social and/or political structure in the survivor's home country? How are the social and political structures similar to or different from those in the United States?

3. What religious belief(s) were prevalent in the survivor's home country? How did religious practices affect the survivor's daily life? Was faith in a higher power evident early in the survivor's life?

4. What were some of the other customs that the survivor remembered from their childhood? How are these customs different from those in the United States today?

5. What values did the survivor learn from their parents and from their childhood experiences?

6. What was the economic status of the survivor's family?

7. Do you think the survivor and his or her family were in survival mode? What indications or realizations did the survivor have growing up about the family's poverty and struggle to survive?

8. What was school like in the survivor's home country? Who provided the education? Was education available for all?

9. At what age did the survivor began to work?

10. What were the survivor's opportunities for an education and a career?

11. Are there any differences between education in the survivor's home country and in the United States?

12. Can you or someone you know relate to the survivor's childhood experiences?

Life Changing Events

1. What change(s) occurred in the survivor's home country that shifted their path in life (e.g. caused them to leave their home country)? What social, political, economic or religious factors contributed to these changes?

2. Do you think it was easy for the survivor to leave their home? Can you identify with any of the trauma they experienced in leaving their family and career, and finding themselves at a survival level?

3. If you were in the survivor's place, would you have risked leaving your home for a different country? Why or why not?

4. What challenges did the survivor face between after leaving their home country and before arriving in the United States?

Life in the Refugee Camps

1. Who managed the camp? How was order maintained? How did the people in charge treat the refugees?

2. Did the survivor and other refugees have access to basic necessities such as food, water, shelter, health care and medicine?

3. Was education offered in the camp?

4. Were religion and refugees' traditional customs allowed in the camp?

5. Can you imagine living in the refugee camp?

6. What do you think helped the survivor and other refugees survive life in the refugee camp?

7. How did the survivor and other refugees get from the refugee camp to the United States? What happened to refugees whose applications were denied?

Life in the United States

1. What preconceived ideas and hopes do you think the survivor had about his or her new country? Were they realistic?

2. What were some of the thoughts and feelings the survivor experienced upon arrival to the United States? Do you think the survivor felt welcome when they first arrived to the United States?

3. What were some of the acculturation challenges for the survivor?

4. Where did the survivor find a place in which he or she finally felt comfortable and welcome?

5. Did the survivor have any marketable skills that helped him or her find employment in the United States?

6. What societal values and customs from the home country helped the survivor to fit into mainstream America?

7. What kind of challenging life experiences has the survivor faced while living in the United States?

8. Did the survivor have anywhere to go for help and support?

9. Did the survivor contribute to the US tax system? Did he or she turn to the US government for any kind of support? Why or why not?

10. How do you think the survivor felt once he or she and family were granted residency in the United States?

11. Do you consider the survivor to be an American?

12. What strengths has the survivor brought to this country and to our society?

13. Do you think that the refugees might feel like they are in a larger refugee camp in the US? Why or why not?

Finding Strength

1. Where do you think the survivor's strength and determination to survive came from?

2. Has the survivor made the transition to "thriver"? What are some of the indications that this transition has or has not happened?

3. Why do you think the survivor chose to work in the community and continues to do so?

Looking Back and Looking Forward

1. How does the survivor view their home country now?

2. What hopes and plans for the future does the survivor have for his or her self, family, community and home country?

Relating to the Story

1. What interested you most about this story?

2. What will you take away from this story?

3. Do you know anyone like the survivor?

4. What action can you take to help the new Americans assimilate into our society?

5. Are there any similarities between the survivors in these stories: their hopes, fears, experiences; and your ancestors who also fled to this country to find a better life?

La Maestra Publications, Inc.
www.lamaestrapublications.org